THE JESUS PRAYER

Per-Olof Sjögren

THE JESUS PRAYER

Translated by Sydney Linton

Foreword by Aelred Squire

London
SPCK

This book is a translation by Sydney Linton of the
second edition of *Jesusbönen* by Per-Olof Sjögren,
published by Verbum Kyrkliga Centralförlaget in
Stockholm, ©Per-Olof Sjögren 1966.

First published in English 1975

SPCK
Holy Trinity Church
Marylebone Road
London NW1 4DU

Translation ©SPCK 1975

Printed in Great Britain by
Bocardo & Church Army Press Ltd

ISBN   0 281 02836 2 paper
       0 281 02856 7 cloth

No matter where we happen to be, by prayer
we can set up an altar to God in our heart.

St John Chrysostom

Contents

ACKNOWLEDGEMENTS

Thanks are due to Faber and Faber Ltd for permission to quote copyright material from *Writings from the Philokalia on Prayer of the Heart*, edited and translated by E. Kadloubovsky and G. E. H. Palmer.

Biblical quotations are from the Revised Standard Version of the Bible, ©1946, 1952, and 1957 by the Division of Christian Education of the National Council of Churches of Christ in the United States of America, and are used by permission.

PUBLISHER'S NOTE

The illustration on the cover of this book is an artist's impression of part of the crucifix at Guldheden Church, Göteborg. It was carved in 1951 by Eva Sp°ngberg but follows the early medieval tradition of portraying the crucified Christ as reigning in majesty from the tree, rather than as dead or dying. The author believes that this crucifix serves as a symbol summarizing the Jesus Prayer because, like that prayer, it brings out both aspects of Christ, as suffering and yet conquering.

Foreword

A book on a practice of prayer identified with Eastern Orthodoxy, written by a Swedish Lutheran dean, translated by an Anglican, and commended by a Catholic priest may well sound like yet another manifestation of the strangely private and not invariably realistic world of specialists in ecumenism. It can only be insisted that there is one, and probably only one, practice of necessarily ecumenical significance about which it is not possible to have theological reserves, and that is the practice of authentic personal prayer.

Among the aids to this practice the Jesus Prayer must be regarded as holding a quite special place. As this unpretentious little book shows, there is something about the very form and nature of the Jesus Prayer that makes its proper use inseparable from a living adherence to the absolutely central tenets of Christian belief. A short but wholly representative quotation from one of those searching letters of the 'Great Old Man' Barsanufius, with which the work of Dom Regnault of Solesmes has made some of us gratefully more familiar in recent years, is a reminder of the peculiar insistence upon truth with and about oneself, which is the mark of all that is most characteristic of the tradition from which the practice of the Jesus Prayer originally sprang, and with which it has remained permanently in touch. Equally reassuring is the indisputable assertion that the common teaching on the doctrine of man, which this practice presupposes, is in unbroken continuity with the biblical view of man as a living unity of whom the body and bodily functions form an integral part. Nineteenth-century Russian masters, like the bishops Theophan the Recluse and Ignatius Brianchaninov, would probably have expressed their caution about the use of a breathing technique in connection with the prayer in rather stronger terms than this book does, but then they would have had in mind something more technically specific and potentially absorbing in its own right than anything which is here described. They might also have felt less at home with the apparent promise of a feeling of unruffled spiritual security in prayer than those nurtured in a Protestant, not to say Scandinavian, tradition of piety which recognizably colours certain pages of this book. But they, like the modest readers they were, would doubtless have pursued it to the end and noted the wiser counsels of its second thoughts on this topic.

In a word, it is impossible not to be happy that another book, written by someone from a younger tradition, should be directing our attention to an older one, which is still very much alive because it unmistakably has its centre in the only ultimate centre of unity, Jesus Christ himself, 'with whom is the well of life, and in whose light we shall see light'. For true prayer not only presupposes a certain minimum of sound doctrine, however unformulated it may be; faithfully pursued, it also inevitably leads to it by the only road that passes beyond all doubt and argument.

Mariakirken, Lillehammer, Norway, 1974   *Aelred Squire*

Author's Preface

The church has been entrusted with a great treasury of prayers. Chief among them is the one Jesus taught to his disciples. The Lord's Prayer is not only the wellspring of all Christian devotion but also an expression of its sum and substance. It contains everything for which prayer should be made and omits nothing deserving of inclusion. It opens the way for the disciple to pray to his Master, and for the child to pray to his Father. It ranks supreme among all the prayers of the Christian church.

Long before the birth of Christ, however, people of faith were praying. In ancient times, for example, they prayed the Psalms of the Psalter. Indeed, the early church continued to use the Psalms extensively, making this hymnbook of the Old Testament its special prayerbook. Ever since the time of the apostles the Christian church has used the ancient words of David as its own. Just as Christ himself prayed the words of the Psalms, so his followers have used these same words to express confession of sin, thanksgiving, prayer, and praise.

Holy Scripture provides us with many other prayers besides the Psalms. There is Zechariah's song of praise called the *Benedictus* (Luke 1. 68–79: 'Blessed be the Lord God of Israel . . .'), Mary's song of praise called the *Magnificat* (Luke 1. 46–55: 'My soul magnifies the Lord . . .'), and Simeon's song of praise called the *Nunc*

Dimittis (Luke 2. 29–32: 'Lord, now lettest thou thy servant depart in peace . . .'). All are part of the rich tradition of prayer in the church. In the *Gloria in Excelsis*, Christian worshippers continue to repeat the song of the angelic chorus on that first Christmas night (Luke 2. 14: 'Glory to God in the highest . . .'). Indeed, many prayers from both the Old Testament and the New are still in use, either in their original form or adapted for private or public worship. For nearly two thousand years now the church's vast prayer tradition has developed from this Scriptural base.

In the church today prayers are often read or spoken. Many prayers in Christian worship, however, continue to be sung—as were the Psalms in the ancient Temple. But the singing of the *Kyrie*, the *Gloria*, or the *Agnus Dei* does not transform them into empty ritual. Whether spoken or sung, these famous lines are expressions of prayer—invocation, praise, intercession, worship, and thanksgiving. Their words are to be prayed, not just with the lips but from the heart.

The focus of this book is on just one prayer in this entire Christian tradition, one of the simplest in form but richest in content of all the prayers in the long history of Christian worship. Though ancient in point of time, the Jesus Prayer does not take long to say: *Lord Jesus Christ, Son of God, have mercy upon me.* In fact, its very brevity may account for its having been so long overlooked by large sections of the church. On the other hand, it has been extensively used and dearly treasured by other segments of Christendom, especially in the East.

Like many other prayers, the Jesus Prayer has a history

all its own, one which goes back as far as the Bible itself. We know that it has been used in its present form since at least the sixth century in the monastery of St Catherine on Mount Sinai. From there it was carried by Gregory of Sinai in the fourteenth century to Mount Athos in Macedonia. As the story has it, during his wanderings on Mount Athos Gregory found many holy men who knew a good deal about prayer as such and many who lived a life of self-denial and meditation, but he found virtually no one who knew the Jesus Prayer. So Gregory instructed the people in this prayer that is prayed 'constantly' (I Thess. 5.17) and the Holy Mountain quickly became— and for centuries remained—a centre for the praying of the Jesus Prayer.

People then began to write down the experiences which accompanied its use, their own and those of others. Gradually a considerable literature on the subject came into existence. During the eighteenth century these writings were brought together and by 1782 a collection of them was published in Venice under the general title *Philokalia*[1]—the 'love of the beautiful'. 'The beautiful' to which the title referred was of course the splendour of the kingdom of God. A decade or so later these Greek

---

[1] Of the original Greek edition of the *Philokalia* from 1782 only a few copies are extant, one at the University of Göttingen and one in the British Museum. A modern edition was published in Athens in 1956–8. Some portions of the *Philokalia* are to be found in J. P. Migne (ed.), *Patrologiae Cursus Completus, Series Graeca* (Paris, 1865), hereinafter referred to as *PG* vol. 147. For practical reasons, however, we will quote from a smaller but more accessible English edition of the more important writings, translated from the Russian by E. Kadloubovsky and G. E. H. Palmer: *Writings from the Philokalia on Prayer of the Heart* (London, Faber & Faber 1951), hereinafter referred to as *Writings*.

writings were translated into Russian, and they circulated widely wherever that language was spoken. Thus did the Jesus Prayer find its way into the Russian Orthodox Church where it received widespread recognition and lasting use.

Strangely enough, it was not until the middle of the twentieth century that this whole prayer tradition was brought over into western Christendom. Perhaps westerners never knew of the prayer at an earlier date. Or perhaps they looked askance at it because of its simplicity, as being beneath the level of intellectual sophistication— and complication—to which their prayer forms were more often attuned. Or perhaps the Roman Catholic and Protestant devotional traditions were both too strongly entrenched to allow for the light oriental touch and spiritual depth of this simple prayer. In any case, it was not until the middle of our present century that the *Philokalia*, or parts of it, began to be translated into German, French, and English, thus opening the West to a way of praying that till then had been limited almost entirely to eastern Christianity.

For many English readers their first acquaintance with the prayer came from *Franny and Zooey* by J. D. Salinger: '. . . if you keep saying that prayer over and over again', says Franny, '—you only have to just do it with your *lips* at first—then eventually what happens, the prayer becomes self-active. Something *happens* after a while. I don't know what but something happens, and the words get synchronized with the person's heart-beats, and then you're actually praying without ceasing.' According to Zooey, 'The Jesus Prayer has one aim, and one aim *only*. To endow the person who says it with Christ-Consciousness.' They apparently learned of this distinctive prayer tradition from a Russian narrative about an unknown pilgrim of the mid-nineteenth century, which was not translated into English until 1930.[1] Thus it took a long time, a journey of nearly two thousand years, but the 'Prayer of the Heart'—as the Jesus Prayer has also been called—finally made its way from the Holy Land, through Sinai, Mount Athos, and Russia, to us in the English-speaking world.

Through these many centuries, of course, the doors between East and West were not hermetically sealed. There was never a total isolation. In terms of content the Jesus Prayer has long been in our midst, though not in the exact form and usage which marks its presence in the Eastern tradition. Christians who in the Lord's Prayer have always prayed 'Hallowed be Thy Name' have always—even in the West—revered the holy name of Jesus and used it frequently in prayer. Pentecostalists, for example, often call out the name of Jesus as a way of expressing a heart-centred relationship with him. And in this book we shall come to see not only how close the western tradition of devotion is to the eastern on this point but also how common has been their heritage of true prayer and worship down through the centuries. The adoption and use of the Jesus Prayer is, for the westerner, no big step.

The purpose of this book is to facilitate the taking of that step, and not just for the spiritually elite but for all

---

[1] See *The Way of a Pilgrim*, tr. R. M. French (London, SPCK 1972; New York, Seabury Press 1965).

people. The Jesus Prayer is not for the specially devout who spend their days in meditation and contemplation, in silence, removed from the world. With its remarkable combination of brevity and fullness it is singularly suited to the busy people of our workaday world, for men and women and youth who have 'no time to pray', not even to get into the mood and spirit of prayer, much less sink deeply into its mysteries. People who have come to know and understand the Jesus Prayer find that it springs to their lips before they are even aware of it, before they even have time to think about it, as surely as the heart within them beats without their taking thought. The prayer simply becomes part of their life, cementing that contact and fellowship with Christ which otherwise is so easily and quickly broken as ordinary people go about their daily tasks 'in the world'. Praying the Jesus Prayer enables the believer to get through the winter of a spiritual ice age. It helps him or her to be and remain a Christian in an environment that is indifferent, even hostile to faith. Indeed, as we examine its content and use in the chapters that follow we shall see that the Jesus Prayer is in itself a veritable school of prayer. It deepens spirituality, furthers devotion of every kind, nurtures fellowship with Christ, and guides us in living out our Christianity in the midst of those with whom we live and work and study and play and worship.

PER-OLOF SJÖGREN

1. *The Jesus Prayer*

There are many forms of wording of the Jesus Prayer. Probably the most common one is:

Lord Jesus Christ, Son of God, have mercy upon me.

Sometimes, after 'have mercy upon me', 'a sinner' is added. Sometimes the words 'Son of God' are omitted.

There are also shorter forms of the prayer. It may be limited to the first part, 'Lord Jesus Christ, Son of God', or again to the second, 'have mercy upon me', though in that case often with the opening word, 'Lord'. In that form it appears in practically all Christian liturgies throughout the world, 'Lord, have mercy upon us', sometimes three times, sometimes nine times, or even, in the Liturgy of St John Chrysostom, forty times. The very simplest form of the Jesus prayer is simply the name 'Jesus'. But all these are to be regarded as variations of the longer form. And that is the one that will be dealt with here.

It consists of two sections:

1 *Lord Jesus Christ, Son of God,*
2 *Have mercy upon me.*

Of these two, it is the latter which is the older. It has been used as a prayer since long before the name of Christ was spoken on earth. It is an Old Testament prayer of great antiquity. To pray for mercy is to pray for loving-kindness. The Latin forms, *miserere nobis*, *misericordia*, convey the idea of tender-heartedness, a heart that is kind. It is this prayer that lies behind many of the prayers of the Israelites, a cry from the burning, fiery furnace, from the pressure of captivity in Egypt, from the long and painful wanderings through the desert—a cry to God that his heart might be open to them in their need, a cry directed to the heart of God. It is important right from the beginning to stress that the prayer for mercy is not a prayer for certain gifts of grace from God, nor a prayer for forgiveness, for strength, for help in the changing fortunes of life, nor a prayer for any particular gift from God, but a cry to God himself, a prayer to his heart, implying: the man who is enfolded in the heart of God needs nothing more, as we find expressed in Psalm 73. 25: 'Whom have I in heaven but thee? And there is nothing upon earth that I desire besides thee', or in the words of a well-known hymn: 'I nothing lack if I am his, And he is mine for ever'.[1] It is an additional advantage and benefit to be able to pray for everything needful, but praying for contact with the heart of God includes all kinds of prayer: confession of sin, thanksgiving, intercession, praise, petition.

The first part of the Jesus Prayer is its New Testament part. In its form, it is a direct invocation, a call. Every prayer begins in this way. In the Lord's Prayer, it is the words 'Our Father' that form this invocation. We find it in our various childhood prayers. Many liturgical prayers begin with 'Almighty and everlasting God' or

[1] Sir H. W. Baker, 'The King of love my Shepherd is', v. 1.

some similar invocation. In the case of the Jesus Prayer, the interesting thing is that it is not the Father who is addressed, but the Son. The Old Testament search for the heart of God finds what it is looking for in Jesus Christ. No one has ever seen God, but God has revealed himself in Jesus Christ. Those who seek the Father find him in and through the Son. 'No one comes to the Father, but by me' (John 14. 6). 'He who has seen me has seen the Father' (John 14. 9). Jesus is the way to the Father, the doorway to the kingdom of heaven. It is evident in the New Testament that when people began to call to him for mercy they believed Jesus to be the Son of God. Bartimaeus, the blind beggar outside the city walls of Jericho, cried out, 'Jesus, Son of David, have mercy on me!' (Mark 10. 47.)

The Canaanite woman up in the district of Tyre and Sidon cried, 'Have mercy on me, O Lord, Son of David' (Matt. 15. 22). The ten lepers in the village on the way between Samaria and Galilee asked, 'Jesus, Master, have mercy on us' (Luke 17. 13). Here were the beginnings of the idea that prayer for fellowship with the heart of God was to be addressed to Jesus. So it was while Jesus was still walking this earth that the Jesus Prayer began to be prayed to him in this way.

At the same time, however, this cry for mercy is one of the most humble prayers ever uttered. It does not make great claims on God but is satisfied with even the smallest token of his love. This is apparent in the original Greek form. *Kyrie eleison* is a request for alms from God; our English word *alms* is actually derived from the Greek *eleēmosunē*, the noun form of *eleison*. Those who are praying do not want to make a selfish claim on the heart of God; they would be satisfied with just a crumb of God's grace, an alms from the Most High. But it has to be realized that an alms from God is never something that God casually tosses our way just to get rid of us. A gift from God is meant seriously. The gift is a sign of his love, of his tender-heartedness. A gift from God binds him to the receiver. By his gift God makes a covenant, or strengthens an earlier covenant. It is from this point of view that we understand how right it is and how important it is that a prayer for God's mercy, for God's alms, be addressed to Christ. When God gave the world the greatest proof of his love, his own Son, he did not send him in splendour, surrounded by all the hosts of heaven, to establish in triumph the kingdom of God on earth. Instead he allowed him to be born in all humility, abased, made sin. He came as man, conceived by the Holy Ghost, born of the Virgin Mary. 'God chose what is low and despised in the world, even things that are not, to bring to nothing things that are' (1 Cor. 1. 28). In this way Christ is God's alms to the world. He is the bread of life that gives life to the world (John 6. 35, 48). He is the way that leads to the heart of the Father (John 14. 6). He is the Samaritan who shows mercy—the loving heart of God—towards the person struck down by the wayside, takes pity on him, binds up his wounds, and brings him to an inn where he can win back his strength until He comes again (Luke 10. 30–7).

This is made even clearer if we analyse the component parts of the first section of the Jesus Prayer: *Lord Jesus Christ, Son of God*. This invocation is nothing less than a capsule summary of Christian doctrine, summing up the whole teaching of the Bible about Jesus.

The name JESUS is the name given to the Son as man. Neither Joseph nor Mary had thought it up, but it was spoken first by the angel Gabriel to Mary at the Annunciation: 'Behold, you will conceive in your womb and bear a son, and you shall call his name Jesus' (Luke 1. 31); and to Joseph in his dream: 'Joseph, son of David, do not fear to take Mary your wife, for that which is conceived in her is of the Holy Spirit; she will bear a son, and you shall call his name Jesus, for he will save his people from their sins' (Matt. 1. 20-1). Both Joseph and Mary were obedient to this message of the angel, and when the child was to be circumcised 'he was called Jesus, the name given by the angel before he was conceived in the womb' (Luke 2. 21).

So it was by the angel that the heavenly Father made known the name of his Son. In this name lies the explanation of his task in the world 'for he will save his people from their sins'. Like all other names, the name Jesus has its special meaning. Nowadays people often miss this, and parents generally choose names for their children for other reasons, according to whether the name is pretty or popular, has been in the family. In Bible times names were chosen on different principles. Parents who call their son John do not always think as Zechariah the priest did when he learned that his wife Elizabeth was to have a son. Both were 'advanced in years', Elizabeth was barren; yet in spite of this she was now to bear a son, 'and you shall call his name John' (Luke 1.13). The name really means 'God is gracious', and is in itself an explanation of how the child came to be born. By his very name John would be a witness to God's grace all through his life.

In the Bible a person's name is not merely a means of identifying the person and distinguishing him or her from others. It is also a key to understanding his or her personality. The name is not just a label attached to the person—it is a characterization, an explanation.

This is particularly true of the name Jesus. Its real meaning is 'one who saves', 'one who is a saviour'. After so many centuries this name has become sacrosanct for us as referring to the Son of God when he became man. It is such a special name that we do not always think about its real meaning. It has become simply the name of a person—a name above every other name, admittedly, but still a personal name. When people ask, What did Jesus come to do?, the question is as meaningless as if someone standing before a blazing house were to ask, why are the fire engines here? The name Jesus means Sáviour, and the Saviour came to save.

So the very mention of the name Jesus opens up the matter of his life and work, the accomplishing of salvation. It is his human name, his high-priestly name, the name under which he bore the sin of humanity upon the cross. He took upon himself our guilt, he died in our stead. He gave his life for us. It was for this purpose that he was born and grew up in Nazareth; it was to this end that he prepared during the three years of his ministry; it was this goal that he achieved when he was sentenced to death and nailed to the cross. That is why Pontius Pilate's writing on the cross was correct : 'Jesus from Nazareth . . .'. The name Jesus alludes to his suffering, his humiliation, his crucifixion, his saving of mankind, for it is by his wounds that we are healed. He is the Lamb of God who takes away the sins of the world. In our place he endured death and opened the way to heaven. He is the gateway to paradise. All this that the Son did comes into focus for the man who mentions the name of Jesus.

When someone strikes a note on a keyboard, it is not just a single note that is heard. An almost incalculable series of overtones and undertones sounds at the same time, giving colour and depth to the main tone. The same thing happens when we mention the name of a person. His whole personality becomes alive to our minds and hearts—in so far as we really know him. The same is true when the name of Jesus is mentioned. The whole of his human personality, the whole of his work of redemption appears before our eyes and reverberates, in the very depths of our being—for anyone who knows him. What we know of Jesus from the Bible comes to life, takes on personal significance, involves us deeply.

But he also has another name: CHRIST. This is a Greek word and it too has a meaning of its own. It means the Anointed One. In any nation there was only one person who was anointed: the king. The Hebrew word for this person was Messiah. So the name Christ does not refer to the humiliation involved in his life and work but to his glorification as King. The very word brings to the fore that aspect of the Son's work which is concerned with his kingship: he comes from God the King Most High, and even during his life on earth he allows the royal glory of the kingdom of heaven to break through— as when he raises the dead, heals the sick, and teaches the secrets of the kingdom of heaven. He himself rises from the dead and ascends to heaven. There he is now enthroned as king; God has given him all power in heaven and on earth. He holds the keys to the kingdom of death and to the kingdom of God. He is Lord over the living and the dead. He is the head of the church. His will must be sovereign over his people, among all who claim to be Christian. His will is to be done in heaven and on earth.

This is made still clearer by the additional name—which again has been in use since the New Testament itself—LORD. This name has a special ring to it. Those who call him Lord have placed themselves under him; they recognize him as their Lord. In his Small Catechism Martin Luther places this word at the very centre of his explanation of the Second Article of the Creed: 'I believe that Jesus Christ—true God, Son of the Father from eternity, and true man, born of the Virgin Mary—is my Lord. He has redeemed me, saved me . . .'. Before the resurrection Jesus is often called Master, Rabbi. After the resurrection he is more often called Lord. At the draught of fishes, for example, when after an unsuccessful night on the lake the disciples cast out their nets a second time at Jesus' bidding—though 'the disciples did not know that it was Jesus'—and then were not able to haul them in for the quantity of fish, it was John who first realized what was happening and said to Peter: 'It is the Lord!' (John 21.7). When Peter understood this he sprang into the sea so as to get to Jesus as quickly as possible. It is both factually and theologically correct that he be called Master both Jesus and Christ. But those who in addition call him Lord thereby declare that they have not only submitted to him and regard him as their Lord, but also that they embrace him in a love that brooks no rivals, that puts him first of all, before anything or anyone else, in accordance with the great and first commandment: 'You shall love the Lord your God with all your heart' (Matt. 22. 37–8, Rev. 2. 4). Those who call Jesus their Lord thereby declare their faith that Christ is alive today, risen and ruling from God's right hand. We cannot be subjects of a dead sovereign or recognize a corpse as our king. However much we may admire the Emperor Augustus, or Alexander the Great, or any former ruler or founding-father of our own country, they are now dead and can no longer reign, so that none of us can now say 'he is my king, my Lord'. But my confession of Jesus as Lord is a direct acknowledgement of his resurrection and ascension into heaven, an open witness that I have at the present time a king on high whom I will worship, love, reverence, and serve above all.

In the case of the Jesus Prayer this is fundamental. The prayer assumes that the resurrection and ascension of Jesus are a reality, and a reality that is still valid. It is of course possible to regard the resurrection and the ascension as historical events belonging exclusively to the past. It is possible to believe in them and yet regard them as *passé*. The ascension is commonly regarded in this way. It is thought of as Jesus' farewell to this world, his departure from this world. In this view the Christians were left alone, alone with their faith, alone with their task to live and work as Christians. Instead, the ascension ought to be regarded as Jesus' exaltation, his advancement to embrace, take in, and rule over the whole world. By the ascension he was set free from the geographical limitations under which he had lived his earthly life, and was placed in a situation from which he is equally available, equally accessible from any point in the world. So to be a Christian today, it is not necessary to travel to Palestine. Admittedly seeing the holy places attunes the heart to devotion and meditation. But Jesus today is at the Father's right hand, and we meet him in the Word and sacraments wherever we happen to be. So his ascension does not mean his going away from the world—on the contrary, it means that he is made available for all the peoples of the world, for their prayers and for their worship. So in the great Orthodox churches the central representation of Jesus depicts him as King, seated on his throne, ruling over heaven and earth. That is where he is now, and it is to Christ here that the church directs her songs of praise. With this in view we understand how essential the resurrection and the ascension are for the Jesus Prayer. The prayer is not directed backwards as it were to a time that is past, to someone who lived two thousand years ago. It is directed upwards, to Christ who is alive and reigning now and who will never die. Paul's words in Romans 6. 9 express exactly what is meant: 'We know that Christ being raised from the dead will never die again; death no longer has dominion over him.'

The additional words *Son of God* in the Jesus Prayer are more than an addition. They are the actual bridge between the first and second sections of this prayer. I call upon my Lord Jesus Christ, who lived here on earth both as Jesus–Saviour and as Christ the King, and who now is Lord and whom I acknowledge as Lord. I call upon him for God's mercy, I call through him to the heart of God, I pray for an alms of God's love to me, for this Jesus Christ is the way to the heart of God, he is God's Son, and he prays for me before the throne of God. He speaks for us sinners before God. He has given his life for us, and having ascended to heaven he still bears his wounds on his body as an eternal memorial before his Father of the work of redemption he carried out on earth, for an eternal deliverance from sins. No one has seen God. He 'dwells in unapproachable light' (1 Tim. 6. 16). But through the Son of God poor sinners can make contact with the Father and with the Father's heart, with him who is love.

This is why the Jesus Prayer is also something of a song of praise, an act of worship, a thanksgiving that there is this Jesus-way to the heart of God, and that we are allowed to tread this way. It is one way to obey the Commandment about 'the name of the Lord your God'; it is an extension of the first petition in the Lord's Prayer: 'Hallowed be thy Name'. It is a summary of the whole gospel: God sent his Son to be a redemption for the sins of men. He let him die and rise again so that today he lives and reigns eternally as Lord over the living and the dead. If we go through the Creed attentively and thoughtfully, we find a summary of the whole content of the Bible. Similarly those who pray the Jesus Prayer thoughtfully find the same: *Lord Jesus Christ, Son of God, have mercy upon me*. Every word is heavy with meaning, every word gives the richest associations to those who know their Bible. Besides being a direct prayer to Jesus it contains also teaching about him, about his work of redemption, his dignity as king, his deity, and his loving mercy.

2. *The Temple in the Heart*

It is fundamental for the Jesus Prayer, as for all prayer, that it be prayed not only with the lips but from the heart. It is not to be superficial words but a turning of the heart to God. What Jesus criticized in the prayers of his people was just this superficiality (Matt. 15. 8–9). Most books on the subject define prayer as the heart's conversation with God.

Exactly what is meant by the word 'heart' may not be so easy to define. Just as in the human body the heart is the organ from which life pours out, so spiritually the heart is the centre of personality—not just the seat of will, feeling, and power, but the essential human ego. Language is not able to say clearly what this is all about. To love someone with all one's heart is more than loving with all one's will or all one's reason or all one's emotion. To be a human being without a heart, a heartless person, is to be inhuman. To be a person with a heart, a good-hearted person, or a person with a heart in the right place is one of the best things that can be said about a person.

The devotional tradition which is the source of the Jesus Prayer has been specially concerned with this concept: prayer as the conversation of the heart with God. Its starting point has been the first instruction in prayer that Jesus gave, in Matthew 6. 6: 'When you pray, go into your room and shut the door and pray to your Father who is in secret.'

This direction by Jesus is regarded not only as a call to go into one's room and pray alone as distinct from praying together in church in services. Jesus' words are also regarded as a call to the individual to go into the chamber of his heart, and there to shut out all evil thoughts so as to be able to pray there, in the heart, to God. St John Climacus, the Abbot of the Monastery of St Catherine on Mount Sinai, who died about A.D. 650, was an authority on the Prayer of the Heart. He writes of the closing of the door in three ways: 'Close the door of your cell to the body, the door of your lips for words to conversation, and the inner room of your soul to evil spirits.'[1]

This thought is developed further; that the heart is to be a temple, God's dwelling place in man, and that in the first place it is the Holy Spirit who is to enter the heart to make it ready for its high purpose. Two ideas are fundamental here:

1) The Holy Spirit and the church always belong together. The Day of Pentecost when the Holy Spirit was poured out on the apostles is often called the birthday of the church. The church as an object of faith is dealt with in the Third Article of the Creed, the Article about the Holy Spirit: 'And I believe in the Holy Ghost, the holy catholic Church'. Luther calls the church the workshop of the Spirit; and the means by which the Spirit works, the means of grace, are those that constitute the church: the

[1] *Writings*, p. 222. Cf. J. Meyendorff, *St Grégoire Palamas et la mystique orthodoxe*, pp. 37–8, in the series 'Maîtres spirituels', Editions du Seuil, Paris, 1959. See also Migne, *PG*, vol. 147, col. 956.

church of Christ is everywhere where the Word of God is preached purely and clearly, and where the holy sacraments are administered in accordance with Christ's institution. Where the Spirit is, there he creates the church. When the Spirit comes upon a person, there he creates a church, a temple in the believer's heart.

The church is not merely an outward phenomenon; it is also a reality of the inner, spiritual life. Paul says: 'Do you not know that you are God's temple and that God's Spirit dwells in you?' (1 Cor. 3. 16).

But this spiritual life has its locus within the body: 'Do you not know that your body is a temple of the Holy Spirit within you?' (1 Cor. 6. 19).

2) It is the task of the Spirit to lead people to Christ and to keep them with him. It is the third person in the Godhead who is to lead people to the second person, who in turn is the way to the first person, the Father. In this way all these three persons are also a unity. For our purposes this means that it is the Spirit who not only creates the temple in the heart of man, but who also makes it a Christian church by eliciting within it prayer to Christ, a call to Jesus. The Spirit not only instructs us in the Word about Jesus, it is also He who prays in our heart to Jesus. Admittedly it is a person's own heart, a person's own lips that formulate the prayer. But it is the Spirit who inspires the person to pray in this way, to call upon the name of the Lord Jesus, to call Jesus 'Lord'.

Of the task of the Spirit to lead people to Christ, Jesus says in his farewell address to the disciples: 'He will glorify me, for he will take what is mine and declare it to you' (John 16. 14).

In his explanation of the Third Article in the Small Catechism Luther says much the same thing:

> I believe that I cannot of my own understanding or effort believe in Jesus Christ my Lord, or come to him, but that the Holy Spirit has called me through the Gospel, enlightened me with his gifts, and sanctified and kept me in true faith. In the same way he calls, gathers, enlightens, and sanctifies the whole Christian church on earth and keeps it united with Jesus Christ in the one true faith.

That the Spirit in this way calls men and keeps them united with Christ does not mean that he just gathers them round him but that he actually links them with Jesus. He leads them into a fellowship, a communion with him, into a unity with him whereby they are no longer outside him but he has united them with himself, entered into their heart, and taken in possession the temple that the Spirit had there prepared for him.

For practising Christians these ideas are not new. Being a Christian is not only having a Christian view of life, accepting certain Christian values and ideals. Nor is it being 'alone with one's beliefs', forsaken by God who sits on his throne far, far away. Being a Christian means being held by Christ, chosen by him, lifted up by Christ as the Good Samaritan lifted up the wounded traveller in his arms. But it also means being directly united with Christ. In baptism the individual becomes a limb or member in the body of Christ. Fellowship cannot be more forcibly expressed. It means being one with Christ, living on him, living from him. So baptism means nothing less than a new birth. The man who was almost dead by the wayside is given new life through Christ. This life is nourished by the Word and by Holy Communion. Baptism is a once-only sacrament because we are born only once. Holy Communion is meant to be used 'often', for once people have been born they need to eat often to maintain life. So in Holy Communion they partake of Christ, they receive there nothing less than his body and his blood, their union with him is further strengthened, and their life receives nourishment from him through this communion. He fills their whole being, their heart and all.

Many Christians at Christmastime have sung a stanza of the well-known hymn 'From heaven above to earth I come', which echoes the main idea of the Jesus Prayer:

Ah dearest Jesus, Holy Child,
Make thee a bed, soft undefiled,
Within my heart, that it may be
A quiet chamber kept for thee.

This comes close to expressing the whole point of this book: it is the Spirit who through the means of grace in the church enters the heart of man and creates there a little shrine, a local church, a personal sanctuary. From here he inspires us to pray to Jesus that Jesus may come and take his temple in possession, so that we may be able to say, in the words of Psalm 11. 4: 'The Lord is in his holy temple.'

It is of great importance that we note this connection between the Spirit and Christ. The Spirit always goes before Christ. In the Old Testament the Spirit appears in many places. Even in creation, before God uttered his creative Word, the Spirit of God was moving over the face of the waters (Gen. 1. 2). The prophets claimed that they were speaking under the inspiration and impulse of the Spirit, the very prophets who were prophesying about Christ (2 Sam. 23. 2). And when the Word was to become flesh, here too it was the Holy Spirit who prepared the way for him, as Gabriel announced to the Virgin Mary: 'The Holy Spirit will come upon you, and the power of the Most High will overshadow you; therefore the child to be born will be called holy, the Son of God' (Luke 1.35). That is why Christ is 'conceived by the Holy Spirit'. The event happened once, once for all. But in the Jesus Prayer this same Spirit in the hearts of men prays that Jesus will come now to the heart that is ready to receive him. The Spirit is eminently 'the Spirit of prayer' prompting people to pray aright. Their own prayer is fumbling, uncertain, weak. But when the Spirit bears it up, it is given its right direction and its right content. Just as no one can of himself believe in Jesus or come to him, so no one can of himself pray to him. That is why 'no one can say "Jesus is Lord" except by the Holy Spirit' (1 Cor. 12. 3), a text that is often quoted by teachers of the Jesus Prayer.

In this connection the early fathers of the church have much to say about the 'tongues as of fire' which on the Day of Pentecost appeared to the assembled apostles 'distributed and resting on each one of them' (Acts 2. 3). The Spirit came to them in this way, in the form of tongues, because the principal work of the tongue is to formulate the word, to fashion and bring it forth. Gregory the

Great, who died in A.D. 604, says in a Pentecost sermon on the Spirit:[1]

He shows himself in the form of tongues of fire
because the Spirit is eternally with the Son
and the tongue is most closely connected with the word.

The Son is the Word of the Father.
And since the word goes forth from the tongue,
the Spirit reveals himself in the form of tongues;
for everyone who is touched by the Holy Spirit
confesses the Word of God, that is the only-begotten Son.

The inner meaning of what happened on the Day of Pentecost is that Christ now comes to the disciples invisibly, the tongue that is the Spirit conveys to them the Word that is Christ. The 'little while' of which Jesus spoke at the last supper and about which the disciples asked him (John 16. 16–19), is now ended, and their fellowship with Christ is once again complete, though spiritual. It is characteristic that Jesus ends his explanation about being absent from them for 'a little while' with a call to prayer and to prayer in Jesus' name: 'Hitherto you have asked nothing in my name; ask, and you will receive, that your joy may be full' (John 16. 24).

Praying in Jesus' name is praying in fellowship with Jesus, in faith in Jesus, in humility and confidence. In a special sense it is to pray the Jesus Prayer from the altar in the temple of my heart, to call upon him and pray that he will come and have mercy on me. No one can pray

---

[1] Migne, *Patrologia Latina* (*PL*), *Sermo 30: In Evangelia.*

in this way of himself, because no one finds Jesus of himself. But the Spirit calls and leads us to him, shows us the way to him. The Spirit is the tongue that speaks the Word into my heart, makes it be born there, take form there, become flesh there. That is why no one can pray 'Jesus is Lord' except in the Spirit, prompted by the Spirit. 'Likewise the Spirit helps us in our weakness; for we do not know how to pray as we ought, but the Spirit himself intercedes for us with sighs too deep for words' (Rom. 8. 26). 'Sighs too deep for words' means the sighs that man himself is not able to, or does not know how to, put into words. The Spirit says them for us. So in the sanctuary of the heart, as in all true worship, it is a matter of 'worship in spirit and truth' (John 4. 24). It is the Spirit who is praying in the heart.

It is essential to note here also the relationship between the name and the person. In the biblical view the name can never be separated from the person. To call upon the name of God means to call upon God. To pray 'Hallowed be thy name' means to pray that God himself may be revealed in his holiness. To trust in the name of the Lord is the same as trusting in the Lord himself. Praying in the name of Jesus is praying in Jesus, in fellowship with Jesus, in union with him. To call upon his name—'Lord Jesus Christ, Son of God '—is to call upon the person himself, in the same way as when we call to a friend or acquaintance we use his name. So the name is not just a means of identifying a person and distinguishing him from all others. It is also a key to the person himself, to his personality, to his heart. In the heart's conversation with God, it is always a matter of heart speaking to heart, the heart of the person praying and the heart of God as revealed in Jesus Christ.

This is most important, for it means that the Jesus Prayer is not only a call to Christ but is a call for Christ. A man in need calls to his Helper, calls for him to come. A sinner prays the Jesus Prayer, for Jesus to come into his heart, have mercy on him, fill him. The goal of the Jesus Prayer is that the Lord shall be in his holy temple 'that your joy may be full' (John 16. 24). Then Jesus' promise of the fullness of joy finds fulfilment. This does not mean that we get all we asked for, though often enough Jesus' promise to hear those who pray in his name has been taken to mean this—as if, provided we 'technically' had used the phrase 'in Jesus' name', we could then expect an exact fulfilment of our prayer. The fullness of joy does not consist of getting all our wishes fulfilled. We do not get it through even the most sophisticated method of prayer, least of all through closing our list of requests with a formula such as 'in Jesus' name'. Rather the fullness of joy consists in having Jesus in our heart. Then we need nothing more. Then the cup of blessedness is full.

In short, when a person studies the Scriptures, goes to Holy Communion, lives as part of Christ's church, then the Holy Spirit enters into his heart and makes it a temple for the Lord. Within the heart he bears witness to Christ and makes Christ alive. From within the heart he calls upon Christ, and that call is a prayer which the Lord hears and answers. He comes and takes possession of his temple.

3. *The Spirit in the Temple*

'So I have someone who prays in my heart.' This discovery can revolutionize a person's life. Christianity is often presented as if it were only teaching, a view of life, perhaps a principle of love, that it is for the individual to put into practice. It is undoubtedly true that Christianity includes all this, but there is more to it than this. Of course it enjoins people to believe certain teaching, to hold a certain view of life, to practise love, but if that is all it did it would be little more than a doctrine of good works. Christianity can never be separated from the church and the Holy Spirit. In the church the spiritual life of a Christian begins with baptism, which means that the individual is made a member of the body of Christ, the fellowship of Christ. A person is not baptized into Christianity but into Christ, the living, risen Christ.

Being a Christian means first of all belonging together with Christ, having fellowship with him, having life from him, the Living One. It is from here that there comes faith and a view of life and love. It is from here too that prayer in the heart is born. It is not a man's own praying, not his own calling upon God. Prayer instead becomes the Spirit's praise to God in a man's own heart. A person becomes a part, a section, a branch of the whole church of Christ—re-echoing praise and gratitude before the throne of God.

If we are to understand the intimacy that marks the Jesus Prayer, we have to enter into the reality of a Christian's intimate fellowship with Christ. So though we run the risk of reducing it to a system, yet for the sake of clarity we can distinguish three stages, three steps in a person's relationship to Jesus.

The first step is taken when a person begins to feel drawn to Christ. We stand at a distance and listen to him, much as the crowds did when he was preaching his Sermon on the Mount. We can stand and watch him when he heals the sick, when he raises the dead. We listen, we take note, but we do not take the step of joining him. We keep watching him at a distance. We may go to church sometimes, we may pray sometimes. We have our own ideas about Christ. Sometimes we understand him, sometimes we react against him. Some people spend their whole lives at this first stage. They would perhaps like to get nearer him, but they do not get the opportunity, or they do not give themselves the chance to do so. Perhaps they have never really wanted to get nearer—after all there are many who draw back from him and do not listen to him any more, do not pay him any further attention (John 6. 66).

The second step is taken when a man begins to count himself one of the followers of Jesus, begins to believe in him and wants to follow him, to walk with him. At this point we have taken the step 'across the line' and committed ourselves to Christ. When Jesus was walking on this earth, it was not only the twelve apostles who went with him day by day on his journeys. We notice this, for instance, when a substitute for Judas Iscariot was to be appointed and they felt that the new apostle was to be chosen from among 'the men who have accompanied us during all the time that the Lord Jesus went in and out among us, beginning from the baptism of John until the day when he was taken up from us—one of these men must become with us a witness to his resurrection' (Acts 1. 21-2). Even today there are many people who identify themselves with this group. They walk with him day by day, they follow in his steps, they look to him as their beloved Master and Lord; but all the time they look on him as someone standing, walking outside themselves. They see him before them, they pray to him on the cross, they meet him in the Holy Communion, they walk beside him. They say: 'Jesus is among us'—but not 'Jesus is within me'.

This third step is taken when we take seriously the words that often occur in the New Testament about the Christian's fellowship with Christ, union with Christ. Jesus himself speaks of it when he calls himself the vine, and his disciples the branches of the vine (John 15). As the branch is united with the vine, is one with it and abides in it, so the Christian is united with Jesus, is one with him to abide 'in me' (John 15. 4). When he talks to the Samaritan woman by the well at Sychar, he speaks of the same inexpressible union: 'Whoever drinks of the water that I shall give him will never thirst; the water that I shall give him will become in him a spring of water welling up to eternal life' (John 4. 14). In one of the letters of John there is a description of the same thing, of how the Spirit acts as intermediary between human beings and Christ: 'By this we know that we abide in him and he in us, because he has given us of his own Spirit' (1 John 4. 13), because all the time it is the Spirit who is leading people to Christ, and who is leading Christ into the hearts of people. It is this fellowship with Christ in which we begin to share in the church. We are baptized into Christ. In the Holy Communion we not only 'meet' him and are at his side, but we 'receive the Body and Blood of Christ',we are united with him in such a way that two become one—and this is why the Lord's Supper has for ages been called communion and compared to a marriage. It is this kind of fellowship which is in Paul's mind when he looks at the cross. He does not stand before the cross and just look at it. He is himself on the cross, together with Christ: 'I have been crucified with Christ' (Gal. 2.20). This unity with Christ is so complete that Christ completely fills him, displacing as it were his own self: 'It is no longer I who live, but Christ who lives in me' (Gal. 2. 20). This is why Paul also endures 'Christ's afflictions' (Col. 1. 24); he suffers with Christ, or Christ suffers in him. At the same time he knows that this fellowship with Christ is not one of the first and simplest planks of Christian faith. It is rather a 'mystery', but it was in order to proclaim this mystery that he had set out on his missionary journeys 'according to the divine office which was given to me for you, to make the word of God fully known, the mystery hidden for ages and generations but now made manifest to his saints. To them God chose to make known how great among the Gentiles are the riches of the glory of this mystery, which is Christ in you, the hope of glory' (Col. 1. 25–7). So this mystery—Christ in you—is not something obvious, open, and comprehensible to all. It is hidden: 'your life is hid with Christ in God' (Col. 3. 3).

This is the greatest secret of the Christian life: that the Infinite can enter into a little human heart, that Christ dwells in a human being's life. Being a Christian is not just having faith in Christ—it is primarily living with Christ, dying with him, rising with him. It is having him in our heart—a hidden life but one that is real none the less. It is from this that faith is born, from this that love goes forth.

This was a secret in the time of Paul—and it may still be a secret today. But this is what makes it possible for us to understand and use the Jesus Prayer not as one prayer among others but as an expression of that inner fellowship with Christ which is the significance of this secret.

'If only we could have lived in the time of Jesus, been able to walk with him, listen to him, see his miracles— how much easier it would have been to be a Christian then.' The modern Christian sometimes thinks and speaks in such terms. It is of course possible to think that way, if we are still in the second of the three stages we have been considering. Because then we are still 'outside' Christ, and it is quite possible that it would indeed have been easier to live as a Christian then if we had seen him alive before our eyes—though the example of the apostles might make us have second thoughts about that. Admittedly they walked with Jesus through those happy, blessed years up in Galilee. But at the cross it was not Peter and his brother Andrew who stood by him. It was not James the son of Zebedee, nor Philip and Bartholomew, nor Thomas and Matthew, the tax collector, nor

James the son of Alphaeus and Lebbaeus, nor Simon the Zealot, nor even Judas Iscariot. His mother was there and a few other women—and of the apostles only John. But anyone who has begun to appreciate the secret of fellowship with Christ, anyone who has entered upon the third stage, knows that he is not separated from Christ, either by two thousand years or by thousands of miles. He knows that Christ is alive today and lives in his own heart through the Holy Spirit. He knows that Christ is not absent but present. He has understood that the resurrection and ascension of Christ have not taken him away from us but have brought him nearer to us. Whereas before these things happened Christ was limited to a particular place and a particular time, after them as Son of God he is present everywhere. As always he follows up the preparatory work of the Spirit; however, he is no longer limited to a province of the Roman Empire but is found everywhere—in the church's means of grace. He is everywhere but he allows us to find him in the word and sacraments. He goes where he chooses, through closed doors to the disciples on that first Easter evening, to travellers on the road to Emmaus. Suddenly he is standing on the shore of Lake Tiberias, but he disappears as suddenly as he came. As he is present everywhere he also enters into the heart of man. It is wrong to idealize the years during which he walked the face of the earth and try to project ourselves back into them. For him his life on earth was no high point—on the contrary it was the day of his humiliation. But after the resurrection and the ascension he entered again into his glory. It is in his exaltation that we meet him today. It is the exalted Lord that enters into the heart of people today. It is to the glorified Christ that the Jesus Prayer is addressed: *Lord Jesus Christ, Son of God, have mercy upon me.*

To understand the Jesus Prayer we have to strip away all false humility. There is a kind of humility that refuses to come this close to God. It belongs to the first of our three stages. A person wants to remain on the sidelines, wants to remain free to say no to Jesus, does not want to to commit himself to him, and least of all to have him in his heart. This is the tragedy of half-heartedness. A person does not dare to give himself to God.

True humility on the other hand is so sincere and takes Jesus so seriously that it rejoices to receive a visit from him. It does not say: 'Who am I that the Lord and Saviour of the world should come to me?' Instead it is as quick as Zacchaeus to hurry home and open the door for Jesus when he now wants to come into the house and be a guest.

In describing how this actually comes to pass we can be guided by the advice of some of the earlier spiritual guides in the use of the Jesus Prayer. For Hesychius of Jerusalem, who died in the fifth century, the starting point is true humility. To that is to be added keen attentiveness, expectancy towards Jesus, and resistance against evil, so that we keep all evil thoughts and desires away from our hearts in order that prayer, the Jesus Prayer, can spring freely from the depth of the heart to Christ.[1]

Barsanufius, another of the writers of the Philokalia, who died in 563 in Egypt, has this to say on the subject of humility:

[1] *Writings*, p. 282 f.

You call yourself a sinner, but in effect you show that you do not feel yourself to be one. A man who admits himself to be a sinner and the cause of many evils disagrees with no one, quarrels with no one, is not wroth with anyone, but considers every man better and wiser than himself. If you are a sinner, why do you reproach your neighbour and accuse him of bringing afflictions upon you? It seems that you and I are as yet far from regarding ourselves as sinners.[1]

True humility is not an attitude worked up in the person who is praying to make himself more acceptable in the eyes of God or those of his neighbours. Rather it is based on a man's realistic view of himself as a sinner. These writers put their fingers on a very sensitive point; they sought to foster total humility. The indwelling of Christ in the soul has to begin with a man recognizing his sin and ceasing to be anything but a miserable sinner in his own eyes.

It is this humility which is the motive for silence. Going into one's room and shutting the door guarantees outward silence. External noise is shut out. Closing one's mouth—in the words of another spiritual guide from the early church—fencing it in with both lips and teeth, guarantees verbal silence, and talking ceases. Shutting the door of the heart guarantees that no thoughts come into the heart from outside.

A great deal is said in this connection about the importance of watching at the door of the heart. Watchfulness against evil must always be keen. The first word of Jesus'

[1] *Writings*, p. 348.

call: 'Watch and pray' (Matt. 26. 41) may be said to refer to a Christian's watchfulness against all evil attempting to penetrate into his heart. When he is with other people, for example, he must still keep watch on this front:

> If you happen to be among people who start to talk idly, leave them and withdraw if there is no special need to remain. But if you must stay, turn your mind to prayer, not because you judge or condemn them, but because you recognize your own weakness. However, if they are well disposed towards you and you know that they are ready to listen to the word of God, try to turn the conversation from empty to useful talk. Tell them, for example, something from the lives of the saints.[1]

We are often warned not to get into discussions and arguments about faith and about God. God does not want his children to discuss and argue. He wants them to be faithful to what they have received in baptism. Heated debate can open the way for evil thoughts and false teaching to enter the heart, with the result that where Christ alone ought to rule, Satan now comes in to challenge his power.

But it is also possible for evil thoughts to come from within, out of one's own heart (Mark 7. 21–3). We must therefore be vigilant not only outwardly but also inwardly. We are warned particularly against worldly and vain thoughts which easily arise while we are actually praying, and which draw attention away from our prayer, away from Jesus to something else.

[1] *Writings*, p. 379.

Against thoughts of this kind fasting is a good defence. A heavy meal does not enhance but actually saps our power of prayer. Eating a modest meal, or even abstaining from food altogether can usually keep our minds vigorous, our intellect clear, and our spirits active—all of which helps our prayer.[1]

Another defence against worldly thoughts is meditating on death. When we are troubled during our prayer by thoughts of someone else, whether by love or hatred of that person, or by the thought of something that in a worldly sense is good and enjoyable, we should carry the thought further and remember that this person, this good thing, this enjoyment, are all subject to corruption and will one day fade and perish. But God will live for ever. Meditating forwards as far as death takes away from worldly thoughts their power to fascinate and distract. It puts them in their proper perspective, reduces them to their proper proportions, so that as we go on with our prayers we see clearly the way ahead.

Thus people who are praying are always to be on watch against the evil which is both inside them and outside. This watchfulness will enable us to reach that total silence which comes when not only our words grow still but also our thoughts and even our desires. In a sense we stop thinking when we pray; we stop having views and formulating ideas. We may well call upon our thought processes when we really need them, but the thoughts as such no longer disturb. We can master them and tell them to keep quiet when that is what we want. We can

[1] St Gregory of Sinai mentions three degrees of partaking of food: abstinence, adequacy, and satiety. *Writings*, p. 78 f.

even come to master our desires, instead of being mastered by them. We no longer desire anything but Jesus. We cease demanding; our hearts are freed from the spasmodic attempts of desire to satisfy its own wishes. We relax; we reach a stage of rest, of openness, receptiveness to Christ.

This openness is usually called attentiveness. The Greek word for 'attention', *prosochē*, means more than simply 'Look out!', 'Be alert'—the sense in which it is used at railway crossings in modern Greece. It means also to stick to the point, to focus and concentrate the mind, to fix one's faculties on the meeting with someone else—literally, as in English, to 'attend'. Attention is used here in the sense of bringing one's heart to Christ, to meet him. It is an active word. I am watchful against evil, but attentive to Christ, open to him. I reach away from evil and reach out to Christ, to receive him in my heart. The call 'Attention, please' spoken on a public-address system means: 'Listen, here is an important announcement.' Mary, the sister of Martha, is attentive in this sense. She has left everything else, she has entered the chamber of her heart and shut the door to worldly thoughts, and is now holding out her heart to Jesus for him to enter in and become her abiding guest. She is not only fasting from food, she is also abstaining from words. She is dumb, practising silence so as to be completely filled with the words of Christ.

At the same time prayer is going on in the heart, prayer to Jesus that he may come. The deepest reason for silence, for my saying nothing, is so that the Spirit may have room to pray in my heart. In church we do not talk about worldly things, we do not sit and chat with one another. We normally sit in perfect silence so that there is space and occasion for prayer, and everyone will be able to pray. When the Spirit prays that Jesus may come, he comes. When Christ comes into our hearts, it is he who speaks, not we. When the King comes to visit, his loyal subjects do not leave him and go right on with what they were doing. They sit at his feet and listen. It is not for us to bring forth thoughts and activities, however good; now is rather the moment for our Lord completely to fill our souls. In the presence of a king it is he who begins the conversation, not I. If he wants to keep silence, then we will be quiet together. But if he wants to talk, then it is for me to listen, and to answer him. My heart and mind are turned wholly to him, whatever he wants. This is how I exercise my *prosochē,* my attention—by attending to my honoured visitor.

There is one further point of importance: when Christ comes into our hearts, he helps us in our battle against evil, and he helps us far more effectively than we could ever manage to help ourselves: *he cleanses the temple.* The unruly thoughts and desires that we fight against, he can rule and govern. Christ's dwelling in our hearts is as realistic as that. Evil will always be gathering new power, springing up afresh, but Christ is 'the gardener' (John 20. 15) who deals with the weeds. He is the Lord of the temple who drives out the money-changers, not just once, but over and over again. The Christ whom we have invited in is no dream Christ, no Christ of memory, but the risen Christ, alive now, the living Lord over heaven and earth. He can command the winds and the waves and he can command the darkest pit of a human heart. He has 'descended into hell', he is not afraid of the Evil One, he joins battle with him in the depths of the human heart, if only he is invited in there. St John Chrysostom says that a Christian must always be calling out: '*Lord Jesus Christ, Son of God, have mercy upon me*',

> so that the name of Lord Jesus, descending into the depths of the heart, should subdue the serpent ruling over the inner pastures and bring life and salvation to the soul. He should always live with the name of Lord Jesus, so that the heart absorbs the Lord and the Lord the heart, and the two become one.

And again:

> Do not estrange your heart from God, but abide in him and always guard your heart by remembering our Lord Jesus Christ, until the name of the Lord becomes rooted in the heart and it ceases to think of anything else. May Christ be glorified in you.[1]

The reference by Hesychius of Jerusalem to humility, attention, resistance, and prayer is not to be taken as meaning that they follow one another in four distinct stages: that we first should exert ourselves to become humble, then move on to attending to Jesus, then quicken our resistance to evil, and finally begin to pray the Jesus Prayer. These four counsels are like the four petals of a flower. The flower consists of all four. Spiritual life grows when they all grow at the same time in our heart, when we know our littleness, when we fight evil,

---

[1] *Writings*, p. 193 f. Migne, *PG*, vol. 147, col. 681.

when we are open to Christ, and when we pray to him. Then he comes, and he does battle against the evil in our hearts far better than we could ever do, and fills our littleness with his fullness.

4. *The Unceasing Prayer*

It has always been taught that the Jesus Prayer is not to be prayed occasionally but regularly, indeed unceasingly. The ancient guides constantly make reference to Paul's words to the Thessalonians: 'Pray constantly' (1 Thess. 5. 17), and to his call to the Ephesians: 'Pray at all times in the Spirit, with all prayer and supplication. To that end keep alert with all perseverance, making supplication for all the saints' (Eph. 6. 18), and also to Jesus' own teaching on prayer, especially as it is described in Luke 18. 1: 'And he told them a parable, to the effect that they ought always to pray and not lose heart.'

Historically, these calls to constant, unceasing prayer have sometimes been interpreted as referring to regular prayer, prayer at routine times, at regular intervals. Even someone who prays morning and evening can be said to be praying constantly. Interestingly enough there is another interpretation of these words which speaks of prayer that is literally unceasing, incessant, and the reference in this connection is to the Jesus Prayer, '*Lord Jesus Christ, Son of God, have mercy upon me.*' This interpretation holds that it is actually possible for this prayer to be prayed unceasingly, day and night, whether a man is awake or asleep, working or resting, alone or with others.

Thus there is a simpler way to construe 'prayer without ceasing' than we have normally imagined. Prayer need not necessarily involve speaking to God, actually making sounds and saying words of prayer to him. There is also something that we can call wordless prayer, being silent before the Lord. When good friends come together they do not need always to be talking to one another. On the contrary, it is one of the surest marks of friendship that they can be silent together and yet be completely at one. They do not need to talk to one another. They still know one another completely, and their hearts are wide open to one another even where no words pass between them. There is thus a kind of unceasing prayer, a state of complete unity, between Jesus and a Christian, and it is quite right to describe this as a kind of prayer without ceasing.

Yet it is not really this kind of prayer that is meant when they say that the Jesus Prayer can become the unceasing prayer. The spiritual guides who tell of the Jesus Prayer really mean that its words are to be spoken unceasingly, constantly, always. But how can such a thing be possible? What do they have in mind?

To find an answer to this question we have to remind ourselves that 'the heart' means not only the 'invisible' heart, the seat of personality, but also the actual muscle, that powerful internal organ with all its chambers and valves. We have to do something quite unusual in western thinking: we have to think of body and soul *not* as separate entities, but think of them together as a unity. We have to think of the heart in a bodily sense in the same way as the Bible speaks of trying the heart and mind (Ps. 26. 2). In many branches of Christianity the spiritual life has been 'spiritualized' to such a degree that it has been separated completely from the body. People have talked about faith as something that exists only in the innermost part of man—like prayer—and that may well have a long way to go before it takes shape in outward action. People have separated faith and works and insisted either that it is enough if we have faith or that the important thing is that we have something in the way of good works to show. Or else people have taken the view that we can live pretty well as we like on the bodily level, if only in the innermost part of our being we have a spark of faith or of love. There are endless variations of this false spiritualizing of religion, and what is common to them all is this unbiblical separation of body and soul.

The *Philokalia* on the other hand views body and soul as a unity. Body and soul together constitute a human being. My body is not an outward, inferior instrument for my soul to use, but it is mine, the only one I have been given in this life, and the form in which I shall one day rise from the dead, though glorified. It is not just a matter of my soul influencing my body and guiding it, but also of my body influencing my soul and being an integrating part of my whole being.

Unless we understand this fundamental idea, we shall misunderstand what follows from it. But it is quite obvious that modern psychiatry has begun to discover something of this connection between body and soul. People are beginning to realize that the 'external' and the 'internal' are much more closely connected with one another than we used to imagine, and that what we are concerned with is nothing less than a unity, the indissoluble unity of a person.

This is the basic view, according to which the Jesus Prayer can be the unceasing prayer, the prayer of the heart. We do not have two hearts, we have only one, and it is located in—our heart. It is this physical heart that is now also regarded as the seat of our personality. The spiritual guides who teach us about the Jesus Prayer take the view that a person can practise praying this prayer in time with the beat of the heart. They link it too, in terms of its regularity, with the breathing in and breathing out of physical respiration:

Then picture to yourself your heart in just the same way, turn your eyes to it just as though you were looking at it through your breast, and picture it as clearly as you can. And with your ears listen closely to its beating, beat by beat. When you have got into the way of doing this, begin to fit the words of the Prayer to the beats of the heart one after the other, looking at it all the time. Thus, with the first beat, say or think 'Lord', with the second, 'Jesus', with the third, 'Christ', with the fourth, 'have mercy', and with the fifth, 'on me'. And do it over and over again. This will come easily to you, for you already know the groundwork and the first part of praying with the heart. Afterwards, when you have grown used to what I have just told you about, you must begin bringing the whole Prayer of Jesus into and out of your heart in time with your breathing, as the Fathers taught. Thus, as you draw your breath in, say, or imagine yourself saying, 'Lord Jesus Christ', and as you breathe again, 'have mercy on me'. Do this as often and as much as you can, and in a short space of time you will feel a slight and not unpleasant pain in your heart, followed by a warmth. Thus by God's help you will get the joy of self-acting inward prayer of the heart. But then, whatever you do, be on your guard against imagination and any sort of visions. Don't accept any of them whatever, for the holy Fathers lay down most strongly that inward prayer should be kept free from visions, lest one fall into temptation.[1]

This is probably that point in the teaching about the Jesus Prayer which has given most offence in the western world—and even led to some ridicule. People have thought that this way of praying is too physical, too primitive, too simple. They claim that the spiritual life obeys different laws, that we cannot breathe it in.

Of course we cannot. This is why it is pointed out repeatedly in the instructions on the Jesus Prayer that this method is only a means to dispose the whole of our being, body and soul, to prayer. It is a way to practise praying without ceasing. Prayer is not meant to be a sporadic occurrence. It must be assured of continuity. It must be given room to live, as surely as there must be room in a person's life for his heart and his breathing. As important as my breathing and heartbeats is my steady prayer to Jesus. To practise this constant praying by mechanically co-ordinating it with the beat of the heart of the work of the lungs is just one way of really providing prayer with this room of its own.

But the practical device is not the important thing. Callistus and Ignatius, joint authors of one section of the

[1] *Way of a Pilgrim*, tr. R. M. French, 3rd edn (London, SPCK 1972), pp. 102–3.

Philokalia, stress the relative unimportance of the mechanics. A state of prayer 'can in no way be achieved solely by this natural method of descent into the heart by way of breathing. . . . This can never be!'[1] It is a work of grace. 'You must know that it is the action of the Holy Spirit.'[2]

It is possible that we are facing here an insight which has certainly not gone unnoticed in western Christianity, but to which not enough attention has been paid. In almost every confirmation book prayer is described as 'the heart's conversation with God' and as the 'breath of the Christian life'. J. A. Bengel comments on Paul's words about praying without ceasing in 1 Thessalonians 5. 17: 'Prayer is the repeated breathing of the inner man, whereby he draws life from God.'[3] But probably all this talk about the breath and breathing of the Christian life has remained—in the West—merely a figure of speech.

The remarkable thing about the Mount Athos Fathers is that they really mean it. They draw in the body and its muscles into a spiritual happening, into prayer. They do not just use their knees to kneel on, they do not just put their hands together in prayer and bow or lift up their heads. They couple together prayer and breathing, and make prayer so fill their breathing that their breathing in and out is woven into an unceasing prayer.

It is possible that we are here facing a function of our bodies that in the western branches of Christianity has been overlooked, but which can now come to life again.

---

[1] *Writings,* p. 195. Migne, *PG,* vol 147, col. 684.

[2] *Writings,* p. 242. Migne, *PG,* vol. 147, col. 768.

[3] J. A. Bengel, *Gnomon oder Zeiger des Neuen Testaments* (Ludwigsburg, 1860), vol. ii, p. 382 B.

We have within us sometimes more than we recognize. The first time we go skiing in the winter, we usually find that our muscles ache. We are using them, after a considerable layoff, in an unaccustomed way, and they remind us of that fact by aching. But after a few more days on the slopes they work without any fuss. Similarly, in the spiritual life, practice makes perfect. Without my really ever thinking about it, my legs routinely carry the entire weight of my body, they carry me, the whole of my person. Without my really ever thinking about it my eyes reflect what is going on inside me, my thoughts, my happiness, my sorrows, my tiredness, my vitality. In the same way my breathing can carry my prayer to Jesus. This does not make it thoughtless prayer. I know that it is there, and at any given moment I find that I may indeed be thinking about it, feeling it, willing it. But just as I have ten fingers, whether or not I go about always remembering that I have, just as I can always know that they are there and use them at any moment, so my prayer to Jesus can be constant in response if not in reflection.

Now it is something of this that makes the Jesus Prayer, the unceasing prayer, convey its blessing to men in ways that they may know nothing about. Through this constant prayer, for example, we find that it becomes easier to pray in general. We do not have to start from scratch every time we pray. The fire of prayer is already kindled at the altar of the heart. Morning and evening prayers are no longer just happenings at certain moments in the daily round. To change the images, they become like the places where a flowing stream (of steady prayer) broadens out to a little lake. And we begin to notice that actually it is not we ourselves who are praying, or we who have been practising this prayer, but that the Holy Spirit has begun to pray in our hearts.

We need not fear that this will lead us into some kind of fanatical Christianity based on personal religious experience. The devil does all he can to stop both prayer and any other work of the Spirit in our hearts. But particularly in times of tiredness we notice when we pray that help comes, though we may not know at first where it is coming from. But gradually it dawns upon us: it is the 'spring of water welling up to eternal life' (John 4. 14) that has begun to bubble up in the heart, cooling us, refreshing us, bringing us fresh life. The walls are thin between body and soul. Concealed in the heart life is growing; the unceasing prayer has got started. It is nourished by the Word and sacraments. The church of the heart is a daughter church of the great temple of the Holy Spirit in the congregation. And it is from there that we draw our resources and our supplies.

We notice too that this inward prayer is accompanied by a certain fresh confidence in taking decisions, a certain sense of security when facing the uncertainties of the future. It is this newfound assurance that is often referred to as the inner testimony of the Holy Spirit. Anyone who lives in this fellowship with Christ acquires with it a certain inner sense of security. The inner temple of our life becomes a stronghold within which we cannot be attacked, an inner world where we can take refuge. Other people, evil thoughts and temptations of all kinds can press in on us. Evil can arise even within our heart, but when we have Christ so near to us, when he really is present in our heart, then we can quickly call upon his help against every kind of evil. Where Christ is, there is life. Christ could not be put to death. He rose again from the dead. Even if we have fallen into sin, we know where to turn, we know where we can seek for shelter, we know whom we can call upon before the throne of grace. And day by day we experience that work of grace which the Lord still performs when he drives the money-changers out of the temple.

5. *The Goal—Christ in Us*

It is not unusual for a worshipper to go to church to meet Christ, and then leave the service with the idea, even the resolve, that now, after this meeting, he is going to live as a Christian on his own out in the world. Granted, the Lord is in his holy temple. But in a rather one-sided way people sometimes think that he is there only, that he awaits his faithful only in the church and then lets them live more or less by themselves for the rest of the week. As a result of this mistaken view the spiritual life is warped from the very outset: on Sundays we live with Christ in the word and sacraments, on weekdays we practice our Christianity by ourselves out among people in the world—where we are to apply Christian principles, guard spiritual values, confess our Saviour before men and bear one another's burdens. The result of this perversion can be a refined and harmful Christianity of works: six days of the week I am to do good, manifest my faith by my works, show what a good Christian I am, and then at last on the seventh day come back to my Master and get my wounds dressed, my sins forgiven, and my strength renewed so that I can go out again on my own, pursuing my lonely struggle in a not very Christian world.

This view of the Christian life, wrong as it is, is not at all uncommon among the faithful. We really have to fight against it, each of us. We have to encourage one another, teach one another, and practise hard in order to live by faith on the weekdays too.

The Jesus Prayer is an excellent aid in countering this wrong view. Its real purpose is to help the individual hold fast to Jesus—whom he has met in church—and to bear Jesus in his heart on the weekdays too, by directing the whole of his attention and prayer towards Jesus. The Jesus Prayer makes life Christ-centred. It emphasizes not how far distant we are from Christ, but how near we are to him. It counts not on his being away from us, but on his being present. It does not assume that a person whose life has its centre in God's word and Holy Communion is on most days far from God and compelled to raise his voice and call from far, far away in the hope of attracting God's attention. Instead the Jesus Prayer assumes that the believing worshipper has accepted the word of Christ and received his Body and Blood, that Christ is in him now, dwelling in his heart, filling him with his goodness. The starting-point for the Jesus Prayer is the affirmation: Christ in us. This is also its goal. By unceasing prayer, by spiritually never letting go of Jesus, we ensure that he abides in us, remains in his temple, the temple of our heart. Of course it is not we ourselves who keep or can hope to keep him with us, because by nature we are perverse and full of sin and evil. Rather it is the Holy Spirit who day by day, hour by hour, unceasingly holds us to Christ.

So as Christians we must always be on the watch against the evil of reducing or denying the presence of Jesus in our hearts. If we have received a gift from the hand of a giver and are now in possession of it, we do not begin to doubt whether we actually have it or whether it is ours. A man who is married to the woman he loves does not begin to doubt whether he is married. He does not begin to long for the chance to marry her—he is already married! A man who is baptized does not need to doubt whether he is baptized. The person who, accepting the word of Christ, has received his body and blood is not to begin doubting the great truth that Christ is in us, dwelling in us.

A fall into sin may remind me that my heart is evil, but this only underscores the importance of Jesus' cleansing it day by day, just as we sweep out our rooms every day. The presence of Jesus in our hearts becomes all the more necessary when a sinner must constantly be hurrying to Jesus, claiming his righteousness, and assuring himself of the grace of God in and through Jesus. Sin is always forcing me away from God, putting distance between us. This distance is dangerous if it is not dealt with at once. For it is this distance that makes the next fall into sin easier, and the next temptation easier to succumb to. But if I hurry at once to Christ to find my righteousness in him, and through him to pray God for forgiveness for my sin, then I can face the next temptation, not lying down but standing on my feet. 'The Lord upholds all who are falling, and raises up all who are bowed down. The eyes of all look to thee.' (Ps. 145. 14–15) The unceasing Jesus Prayer, continuing even when I am not articulating it or consciously reviewing it, even when I am asleep, becomes at this point a weapon of the Spirit to drive me at once to my Saviour and direct my attention constantly to him so that my eyes are ever turned upon him, waiting for him.

Now if Christ dwells in a person's heart, the next question is: What is he doing there? He can either rest there or he can work there, as on the morning of creation. When God enters into the heart of the believer God's work and God's rest are both transported, relocated, implanted in that heart.

Having God's rest in our heart affords the greatest security and bliss. It is like having a little Bethlehem inside ourselves, a stronghold in which to take refuge, not just to shut ourselves in, but to be safely out of Satan's way, where we can dwell in peace and quiet with Jesus. Many Christian hymns speak of this blessedness, for example, 'Come, Holy Ghost, our souls inspire', based on the ancient *Veni, Creator Spiritus*:

Keep far our foes; give peace at home;
Where thou art guide, no ill can come.

They reflect the sweet bliss of which one of the writers in the *Philokalia* speaks: 'Who will explain the sweetness of honey to those who have not tasted it?'[1]

We find here another reason for a Christian's silence. Silence is not just a kind of ascetic discipline which we lay upon ourselves. It is not a clamp over our lips such as a schoolteacher might impose in calling for silence in the schoolroom. Rather silence means freedom from the bondage of words, freedom from the constraints of thought and desire, freedom from the compulsion to go on talking and thinking up ideas and adopting viewpoints and

[1] *Writings*, p. 243. Migne, *PG*, vol. 147, col. 768.

feeling desire—or repressing such feelings. We often read of this in one of our communion hymns:

Let all mortal flesh keep silence
And with fear and trembling stand. . . .

At last all our inner drives to think and desire and form words can come to an end. The whole person can rest and be at peace—and worship Christ. The way to this freedom from self most commonly lies in the imposition upon ourselves of some outward discipline. But its aim and purpose is that we shall be set free to worship.

To describe this resting with Christ, it is common in devotional literature to draw a parallel with the years of silence in Nazareth, the thirty years that Jesus spent with Mary, Joseph, and the rest of the family prior to his public ministry. These are characterized as years of the Lord's rest compared with the briefer time that followed and was so filled with the Lord's work. Very few descriptions of the earlier period are preserved for us. We have much more from the period of almost unresting ministry.

Similarly, Christ rests in a person's heart, imparting a sense of inner peace in the midst of suffering and of toil. From within Christ gives times of rest to body and soul. The demand to achieve and produce can become a heavy burden unless it is balanced by this gift of stillness or inner freedom. Just as surely as Sunday comes along after all the other days of the week, so Christ makes times of rest alternate with times of labour. These times of quietness in a person's life are in no sense a matter of laziness or slackness. They come as a pause of solace, as creative peace. It is important that we learn to recognize such moments. The desire to act, the pressure to produce can sometimes make modern people resent this inner rest instead of enjoying it and experiencing renewed strength while it lasts. Now and then Christ sends times of quiet like this in a person's life, times of preparation for re-charging our batteries. For we are going to need strength for the work to which Christ is leading us.

This work has been variously described. For our pur-poses perhaps the simplest way to describe it is to link it with Jesus' own work, to those two sides of his nature to which the Jesus Prayer refers: his work as man, as Jesus, and his work as Son of God and King, as Christ.

When the prayer is addressed to Jesus, it is his passion that looms large before the inner gaze of the person pray-ing. In prayer he is looking at his Saviour. But he looks at the Saviour's sufferings not as something which hap-pened once in the distant past. He knows that Christ did suffer and die, the Christ who has also risen again and now lives in his own heart, but he knows too that he is himself a part of Christ's body, dedicated by baptism to suffer and die—and to rise again—with Christ, like Christ: 'Do you not know that all of us who have been baptized into Christ Jesus were baptized into his death?' (Rom. 6.3).

So suffering is not just one item in a long list of Chris-tian articles of faith that a person accepts theoretically with his intellect. It becomes also an expression of one's inner fellowship with Jesus, the suffering Saviour. To have Jesus in one's heart is to expect to suffer with him, even, to use Paul's expression, to be 'crucified with Christ' (Gal. 2. 20). Jesus' suffering on the cross is over, having taken

E

place once and for all, but the members of his body still have to suffer with him.

The Passion of Jesus, however, did not begin on the cross or in the garden of Gethsemane. It began when he became man. That is why the whole of his human life is marked by suffering. He experienced the pains of birth, the growing pains of childhood, the pain of temptations in the wilderness and on the pinnacle of the temple and on the mountain top, the pain of heavy daily toil among all the sick and afflicted people in Galilee, the grievous pain that assailed him in Gethsemane, threatening even to overpower him, the fear of dying, of death by a cross, and finally the pain of actual death, both physical and spiritual, revealed in his words: 'My God, my God, why hast thou forsaken me?' (Mark 15. 34).

Whoever prays the Jesus Prayer must count on having to face this pain, this suffering. It is part of the life of Jesus, both then and now. What we have to guard against above all is idealizing our fellowship with Jesus. This happens all too often. People are used to looking up at the figure of the Crucified as something exalted, beautiful, attractive. People speak of his 'blessed' passion, an appropriate term—true in so far as the passion and death of Jesus brought blessing and bliss to mankind, provided we realize that the actual suffering was anything but lovely. Suffering is always painful. A person's way of facing suffering may inspire us, may indeed be beautiful to see, but in itself evil is harsh, hard, and harrowing. Death is not beautiful; it is the extinction of life. The Lord came to earth to die. And it is this death, drawing slowly but surely closer every moment from Bethlehem to Golgotha, that by Word and sacrament now flows into the heart of the believer. It is fellowship with this side of the life of Jesus that is made real when we pray the Jesus Prayer: *Lord Jesus.* . . . It is reassuring to know that Jesus foretold exactly this: 'It is enough for the disciple to be like his teacher, and the servant like his master. If they have called the master of the house Beelzebul, how much more will they malign those of his household. So have no fear of them' (Matt. 10. 25–26). In itself this prediction does nothing to soften the edge and pain of the suffering, but it does help to explain it—other things as well. The frequent exhortations in the *Philokalia* not to argue, not to dispute about the faith with outsiders, not to struggle against those who oppose it—all are explained by the silence of Jesus before Pontius Pilate: he kept quiet before his accusers.

Here too we get our reason for fasting. Even fasting is not just an outward discipline, laid upon us to increase our powers of resistance and make our spirit freer vis-à-vis the body's demand for food. Fasting is sharing Christ's suffering in the wilderness at this point too.

But it is not only his suffering that is part of Jesus' work as Saviour. His teaching and his preaching are also part of it. To have Jesus in our hearts is to have a Master within who speaks as no man ever spoke (John 7. 46). The preaching of Jesus is not spoken only in the churches, it is not written only in the Bible, but it is now also written upon my heart by the finger of the Holy Spirit (Jer. 31. 33). In other words there is also a pulpit in the church of my heart from which Jesus preaches his word—to me. The Word of God, the teaching of Jesus, is not just a general word spoken to the whole world. It is a specific word directed personally to me. Jesus speaks in my heart to me.

It is this that gives point to our private reading of the Bible. I read the Bible not just to learn what is written in it, but to hear what Jesus is saying to me, and to be able to distinguish his voice in my heart from what my own heart is saying, thinking, and demanding—for my own heart never stops speaking. It is by hearing Jesus speak through the Bible that my heart, like my conscience, becomes instructed in the Word of God. Gradually I begin to be able to distinguish between Bible teaching and false teaching, between what God is saying and what my own heart or other people are saying. It begins to be possible for me to sort out the words that come in an often overflowing stream from my heart.

At the same time various situations make certain Bible passages come to life for me, in the same way as when Jesus was tempted in the wilderness and rejected all three temptations with quotations from the Bible. Similarly in my life Christ uses special quotations from the Bible when I am tempted. When he sees I am in danger he comes to my aid and gives me the right word at the right moment. In this way he helps me to fight against temptations, to endure suffering, to beat back despair, and to overcome the fear of death. He has gone through all of these himself. His word becomes a lamp to my feet (Ps. 119. 105), my heart becomes a treasury of his word, a treasury from which Jesus himself brings out just what I need in order to find the narrow way forward in my daily living.

Reading the Bible is not an imposed discipline, something one *ought* to do as a Christian. Instead it becomes the voice of Jesus, daily comforting, teaching, encouraging, and warning me. When I am tempted to steal I am reminded of the commandment against it, and I suddenly realize that it is not I myself who happen to 'remember' it just in the nick of time, but Jesus who speaks the commandment to me in my heart. In this way I am reminded both of how near Jesus is to me in temptation and of the passages in the Bible which forbid the sin I was about to commit. I know that I am not just being watched—I am being watched by my best friend, who gave his life to save me from sin. I am not alone in temptation. Jesus is standing by my side.

Take another example: a person notices that he is getting caught up in real hatred of somebody else. Bitterness and self-pity increase the hatred. Then 'he remembers' a passage in the Bible: 'Love your enemies and pray for those who persecute you' (Matt. 5. 44). He suddenly understands that he did not just 'happen' to think of this passage—it was the Saviour dwelling in his heart who brings this word into his consciousness, brings it forth from the treasury in his heart and holds it up for him to consider and think about, so as to save him from hatred and enmity and to show him the narrow but only way out—the way of praying and loving.

There are times when Jesus makes a person wait, when he does not talk but keeps silent. Jesus is no general information office. Sometimes he neither speaks nor acts, so we have to sit down and wait, as at the wedding in Cana: 'My hour has not yet come' (John 2. 4). A Canaanite woman once pursued him a long way without getting an answer, even though she prayed a prayer much like the Jesus Prayer. 'But he did not answer her a word' (Matt. 15. 23). This is why it is so important to cultivate a capacity for waiting, for remaining attentive and open as we wait for Jesus to take action. This was what Mary urged the servants at Cana to do. This is what James urges: 'Be patient . . .' (Jas. 5. 7). This is what is meant by directing our attention to Jesus.

One further point needs to be made clear: I remain silent in order to allow him to speak—him alone. For it is not only my evil thoughts and desires that must be silenced. It is also those thoughts I produce with the best of intentions, my ideas about Jesus, my interpretation of his sayings, even my faith in him. In other words it is a very subtle temptation to believe in our own faith instead of believing in Jesus himself. Often we form a view of Jesus, starting perhaps even in early childhood, and then we build the whole of our Christian life on this early understanding in the belief that we are thereby building on Jesus himself, on the rock itself. And when the tests and storms of life begin, we notice perhaps that our 'faith' does not hold. With disappointment, perhaps in despair, we see our 'faith' collapse. We may even think that the whole of Christianity has gone bankrupt. But what has happened may turn out instead to be very beneficial. Our own homemade faith has broken down. God has entered my heart and pulled me down from the pulpit I had erected there. He would enable Jesus alone to speak from the pulpit of my heart. So he silences my own interpretation, my own Christian theories and teachings in order that he himself at last can be allowed to speak in his own temple. The disputatious preacher has been dismissed, and it is for Jesus alone to speak now.

The Jesus Prayer, however, is directed not only to Jesus the Saviour but also to Christ the King. It is this exalted side of his being that appears most clearly in his divine speaking, in his miracles, clearest of all in his resurrection, his ascension into heaven, and his being seated on his throne in heaven. *Lord Jesus Christ, Son of God, have mercy on me.* The Apostles' Creed combines these two sides—Saviour and King—in the Son of God. It is the same Son of God who was conceived by the Holy Ghost, born of the Virgin Mary, suffered under Pontius Pilate, was crucified, dead, and buried, the same Son of God who descended into hell; who on the third day rose again from the dead, ascended into heaven, and sitteth on the right hand of the Father. His majesty is revealed most clearly in his glorious resurrection, his ascension into heaven, and his taking his seat on his heavenly throne. That is where he is now. And to that point, to Christ at God's right hand, the whole of the church's praise and worship is addressed. At the same time, however, he cannot be kept at a distance, he cannot be shut out. In this respect he shares in God's nature of being present everywhere, through the Spirit. When the Spirit is allowed to lead a person where he will, he leads Christ into that person's heart, the same Christ who is the exalted King. In the temple of our heart there is not only a pulpit from which the Lord speaks and an altar on which he suffers. There is also a bishop's throne on which Christ as the true

Shepherd and King presides and from which he exercises his power in our life (1 Pet. 2. 25).

This is what makes Christianity such a vital, living, contemporary thing. To be a Christian is not to grasp in faith a Saviour who died two thousand years ago. It is not to rest in the past, sustained by a memory of Jesus. To be a Christian is to live in fellowship with a risen Messiah, who is ascended into heaven and seated on his heavenly throne, a Messiah whose kingdom is not of this world, yet includes the hearts of those who acknowledge him as their king. That is why the resurrection is an absolute precondition of all prayer, including the Jesus Prayer. To call Jesus 'Christ' is to honour him as Messiah, as the Anointed One, the Lord and King of our lives. When in the Lord's Prayer we pray 'Thy kingdom come', we are praying that this kingdom of his may be increased, may grow. Anyone who prays that petition must first of all see to it that he does not sabotage the coming by disobedience within that province of the kingdom which is his own heart. The word 'Lord' in the Jesus Prayer is my humble acknowledgement that the risen Messiah is not just king over others, but my king also, that he is 'my Lord'.

What the indwelling of Christ in our heart is to mean is quite impossible to foresee. He is our Saviour and divine preacher, he is our King and Lord. As such he is at work. As such he is also at rest when he so pleases. He cleanses the temple, he drives out daily the evil that springs up there like weeds. He receives our worship and praise, he carries us through suffering and trials. He raises us up when we have fallen. He warns us, comforts us, encourages us, gives us joy. In all this he is our best friend. 'Who shall separate us from the love of Christ?' (Rom. 8. 35).

At the same time he is inscrutable. No one can foretell how he will act. No one can say: If Jesus had been living now, he would have said this or that, he would have acted in such and such a way. To speak like that would be to reflect the belief that Jesus is not living now (that we do not believe in the resurrection, or that we regard it as something that happened once in the distant past but has no relevance for the present time). It would mean that we believe we can formulate new sayings and invent new actions of Jesus ourselves, today—an expression of over-weening pride. No, if we live with Jesus in our heart, we know much about the Jesus of today, what he says and what he does now, for he himself makes it clear to us. But over God's revelation of himself in time there is often a veil of incalculability, of inscrutability. Even Isaiah foretold that 'his name [God himself] will be called Wonderful Counsellor . . .' (Isa. 9.6), a name that betokens God's wonders, God's miracles. He astonishes us, he surprises us by his wonders—today as surely as when Jesus walked this earth.

Experiencing this side of God's being can also make us afraid: If God is like that, he might do anything. It is worth remembering that questioning along these lines has always accompanied the use and experiences of the Jesus Prayer. Gregory Palamas, one of the great four-teenth-century leaders of Eastern Orthodoxy on Mount Athos, fought a hard and victorious struggle against the Barlaam who was declared a heretic, whose main thesis was that God was impossible for us to get to know.[1] According to Barlaam's view, prayer can become a crying out into the void, a cry with no destination, and this view is really a form of Christian agnosticism: no one can know anything about God. Gregory Palamas on the other hand maintained that God is indeed 'wonderful', but that he has revealed himself in Jesus Christ and that a sinner can make contact with him and get to know him through the church's word and holy sacraments. God's being 'wonderful'—inscrutable— does not mean that it is impossible to get to know him. But some parts of the knowledge of God are too high for men to receive or understand. The kind of Christian agnosticism Barlaam represented makes prayer more or less meaningless. It leads people to apathy and despair, to indifference and neglect of the spiritual life. So when Barlaam's teaching was declared to be heretical, the decision marked a clear line against the spiritual slackness and decadence of the Renaissance, while at the same time making clear that the Jesus Prayer is based on the revelation of God in Christ: He has shown himself as Saviour, as King and Lord and as one who has mercy on sinners. This much knowledge about God it is possible for us to attain. On this knowledge the Jesus Prayer is based. And this is enough for salvation.

[1] See J. Meyendorff, *St Grégoire Palamas et la mystique orthodoxe*, p. 88 ff.

6. *The Jesus Prayer and Other Prayers*

It would be easy to get a wrong idea about the Jesus Prayer as being the kind of short-cut to God that can make all other prayers unnecessary. He who has Jesus in his heart might well think that from then on the Jesus Prayer is enough. But it is important to point out that this is not true. The Jesus Prayer can never be a substitute for prayer together in the congregation on Sunday or for morning and evening prayers in the privacy of the home.

This is made abundantly clear by many writers in the *Philokalia*. Their instructions assume that those who pray the Jesus Prayer also go to church regularly, receive Holy Communion frequently, and say their own prayers daily—and nightly too for that matter. It is inconceivable for the Mount Athos Fathers that one pattern or order of devotion should replace another, or that one means of grace should be allowed to replace another. The Jesus Prayer does not make Holy Communion unnecessary. On the contrary, we have already seen how clearly it is assumed that the person who has Jesus dwelling in his heart has been receiving his Body and Blood in Holy Communion. The presence of Jesus is not something that we have at our disposal, that we can take for granted, that is ours simply for the wishing. Jesus comes of course when we ask him to come, but he comes in the way he has instituted: in the Word, in Baptism, and in Holy Communion. The authors of the *Philokalia* have not fallen prey to the temptation of falsely spiritualizing the spiritual life. The whole of their world, their entire faith is firmly rooted, deeply rooted and grounded in the routine life of the church, in word and sacrament. They look on the various means of grace as a banquet, a feast where we can partake of every dish. This is how the Lord fully satisfies our hunger with his grace.

In one of their treatises, for example, Callistus and Ignatius approvingly quoted St Basil the Great, who died in 379:

> It is good and most useful to have communion every day and to partake of the Body and Blood of Christ, for Christ himself says clearly: 'Whoso eateth my flesh, and drinketh my Blood, hath eternal life' (John 6.54).[1]

> The greatest help and assistance in purification of the soul, illumination of the mind, sanctification of the body and a Divine transformation of the two, as well as in repulsing passions and demons and, above all, in transubstantial union with God, in joining and merging with him, is frequent communion in the holy, pure, immortal and life-giving Mysteries—the precious body and blood of our Lord Jesus Christ, Our God and Saviour—approached with a heart and disposition as pure as is possible for man.[2]

All that was said in the previous chapter about the resurrection as the obvious premise for the presence of Christ in the soul applies also to Holy Communion. It is

[1] *Writings*, p. 263. Migne, *PG*, vol. 147, col. 800.
[2] *Writings*, p. 259. Migne, *PG*, vol. 147, col. 793.

with the risen Christ, seated now as king on the heavenly throne, that we are united in this sacrament. The *Philokalia* quotes from a discourse of St John Chrysostom:

In partaking of the body of the Lord and in drinking his blood let us firmly remember that we are partaking of that body which sits on high and which the angels worship, a body which stands nearby the imperishable power—that very body we eat.[1]

The Jesus Prayer assumes that Sunday by Sunday we share in the regular use of the eucharistic prayer and in other prayers throughout the day, at least in morning and evening prayer on weekdays. Without this framework of a total grounding in prayer the unceasing prayer would be left, figuratively speaking, in the air.

Careful analysis of the traditional prayers of the Communion service shows how well they blend with the Jesus Prayer, or how the Jesus Prayer blends with them. They certainly do not compete with one another. Early on in the service we usually pray:

Lord, have mercy upon us
Christ, have mercy upon us
Lord, have mercy upon us

This is quite simply the Jesus Prayer. We find the same words often in the so-called Liturgy of St John Chrysostom, the soil from which the Jesus Prayer grew, for there the *Kyrie* is repeated over and over again throughout the service.

[1] *Writings*, p. 261. Migne, *PG*, vol. 147, col. 796.

An ancient song of praise that in many churches follows immediately upon the angels' song, 'Glory be to God on high' is another variation that enlarges upon the Jesus Prayer, especially in the lines addressed to the Lamb of God:

We praise thee, we bless thee, we worship thee, we
glorify thee, we give thanks to thee for thy great glory,
O Lord God, heavenly King, God the Father Almighty.
O Lord, the only begotten Son, Jesu Christ,
O Lord God, Lamb of God, Son of the Father,
that takest away the sins of the world,
have mercy upon us.

The publicly read Gospel lesson is clearly the word of Jesus to the assembled congregation, but also to the heart of the individual. The Creed is addressed not only to the Father but also to 'Jesus Christ, his only Son, our Lord . . .' and of course to the Spirit. Throughout Christian worship we are constantly reminded of the spiritual reality on which the Jesus Prayer is based.

The familiar words of John the Baptist, the Agnus Dei, are really in their content a variation of the Jesus Prayer: 'O Lamb of God, that takest away the sins of the world, have mercy upon us.'

So the prayers of the liturgy are in line with the Jesus Prayer. Naturally they are fuller and more encompassing in scope, but they in no way exclude the Jesus Prayer, nor does the Jesus Prayer exclude them. They do not compete or conflict. They work together.

Analysis of Matins and Vespers and other daily morning and evening prayers shows the same pattern of parallelism and overlapping which in this small book we cannot trace in detail. For our purposes it is enough to say that the prayers meet and mesh like good friends rather than competitors. Together they form a rich and full treasury—a liturgical feast of resounding praise and prayer, in church and out, from morning till night, at the beginning and ending of the day, filling with unceasing prayer, the Jesus Prayer, all the days and moments and intervals of the entire week.

To describe the relationship between all these forms of prayer, the soul has been likened to a garden. To protect it, the owner has erected a fence of strong posts firmly fixed at regular intervals. Connecting the posts are an upper wire and a lower wire, with a fine-mesh network between them. The fence represents prayer. The sturdy posts fixed at regular intervals are the Sunday services, the structural framework of the devotional life. The upper wire is morning prayer, the lower wire evening prayer, and the fine-mesh network between is the unceasing prayer, the Jesus Prayer. When all three are in place, the garden of the soul is protected. If there is a break at any point ravenous beasts can get into the garden and do damage. Temptations can make their entry to the soul and spoil its growth. So Sunday religion alone is not enough; however strong the posts, they do not of themselves make a fence. Nor can a garden be protected only by an impressive network of wires for the network itself has to be fixed to unmoveable posts. Living as Christians on our own without the worshipping community does not work. We need the Sunday services in the congregation on which to 'hang' our Christian life. And between our morning and evening prayers we need to talk often to Jesus, to think of him, to be constantly in contact with him (whether or not we are constantly conscious of this contact). Modern life faces us so often with unexpected risks, temptations, and dangers, that we need to be able to call our Master without long preparation and delay—this is the unceasing prayer, the fine network between our regular morning and evening prayers. There is no need to wait for evening to call our Lord; we can do it at once, at any time.

So the Jesus Prayer, the unceasing prayer, is in no sense in competition with other kinds of prayer. On the contrary, it complements them. Our prayer life consists of regular worship in the congregation each Sunday, daily prayer at home, and unceasing prayer everywhere. These three taken together provide the protection and nurture that fosters the growth of the spiritual life.

7. *The Jesus Prayer Today*

By this time you may well be wondering: Is the Jesus Prayer really for me? With its roots in the Bible and its acceptance primarily in the monastic life of Eastern Christianity, can it be used by modern people today in the western world? People of course use the prayers that suit them best. The prayers they commonly hear in church come easily to the lips; prayers of their own devising often mark their morning and evening devotions. Christians tend to use whatever best expresses—and builds—faith in Christ.

The Jesus Prayer has always spread beyond the areas of its earlier acceptance and been gratefully received in new places precisely because it has served a need, especially for people who really want to 'pray without ceasing'. It remains therefore to add here some reflections on its universally acknowledged value as a devotion of the Christian heart today.

The Jesus Prayer is short. It can be prayed in a fraction of a second, literally 'in one breath'. No long preparation is needed. There is no need to settle down and get ready, to sink into silence. It can be prayed in the midst of other activity, while you work, whenever you are tempted, even in the middle of a conversation. I do not have to finish what I am doing before I can start praying. The

Jesus Prayer lets me pray whenever I need to call upon the Lord.

This is not to say that the Prayer has no meaning, that it is thin in content and spiritually poor. On the contrary, it is highly concentrated. It puts me in immediate contact with Jesus the Saviour, Christ the King, the Son of God, my Lord, and it asks him to be merciful to me. Every word in it is full, heavy with meaning. It opens the door to the deep treasure chamber of grace. It is not just a general calling upon God. It is addressed specifically to the Son of God who suffered and died, who rose from the dead and is now living and reigning, who is my Lord, and who can and will be merciful to me. It is a prayer from the believer's heart to the heart of God in Jesus Christ.

Strictly speaking, it can be further shortened—to a single word. Sometimes it is enough just to use the name, JESUS. When we talk to one another in daily conversation, we do not always use full names, both Christian names and surnames. In fact we usually use just one name in speaking to persons who are close to us. And the same is true here. Just to whisper the name, speak the name, call the name, breathe the name of Jesus can bring a soul encouragement, warning, victory over evil, salvation.

A name has so many associations for anyone who knows the person it belongs to. 'It is like looking at a snapshot from a recent trip. For those who made the trip together the picture brings back all the events connected with it. This is why we have photographs taken of our loved ones, because we want to be reminded of them, think of them. The pictures bring us joy even if the people themselves are absent. In the same way, a person's name serves as a bridge between me and that person. I can whisper the name to myself, and the name alone brings back to life all the meaning and joy I associate with that person.

This is even truer when we name the name of Jesus. All that Jesus said and did when he was here on earth, all that he is today, where he sits at God's right hand, all that he has done and is still doing day by day for me personally and for the whole of our world—this is brought into focus when the name Jesus resonates in our ears. This backdrop gives colour and depth to the picture in our minds when we pray this single word of prayer, JESUS.

But this short prayer is not just a way of concentrating thought on my Saviour. It is really a prayer to him, a heart's communication with him. Just as I call to a person by saying his name, so this short form of the Jesus Prayer is a call, a cry to Jesus, and he answers it when and as he chooses. Just saying the name of Jesus in Spirit—that is to say, in concert with God's holy church—is one way of getting in touch with Jesus himself.

In the tight schedule of a busy day we find how useful the Jesus Prayer can be, indeed, how necessary. Many committed Christians today complain how difficult it is to keep in touch with Christ in daily life. It is wonderful to be able to meet him in church. At home, with Bible or prayer book open, we can sink into his presence, seeking his mercy and his grace. But when the church service is over, when our time of prayer comes to an end, all the duties and tasks and demands and people come pressing in on us again and the stillness of our time with God is blown away. The speed of modern life is so great, our nerves tense, and the struggle to live as a Christian in all of this becomes unbearably difficult.

It is here that the Jesus Prayer comes as a welcome help to the individual Christian. It enables us to maintain contact with Christ. Even in the tightest of schedules there come those momentary breaks, those one- or two-minute pauses which arrive as an unexpected gift. I miss my train or bus: instead of using the few minutes I have to wait for composing in my mind an angry letter to the newspaper about the deplorable state of our public transportation, I can quietly reflect; I can make use of those few minutes to think about Jesus Christ, the Son of God, my Lord, and to ask him to be merciful to me.

Or again: I have to go and see my boss, and I know it is not going to be easy. While I nervously await the critical moment I can use the intervening seconds or minutes to pray the Jesus Prayer. If I have a long wait, I can dwell on the name Jesus and think of what the Gospels say about his being a Saviour, or I can dwell on his name Christ and think of how he is at God's right hand, looking down on me in mercy.

Or again: I meet someone who is angry and either vents his fury on me or treats me with cold and bitter sarcasm. Instead of feeling defenceless, or trying to hit back with the same weapons, I can pray the Jesus Prayer in my heart and there perhaps keep peace, even letting the inner silence spread to the silence of my lips.

Or again: I come home tired after a long day's work, worn out, exhausted, almost in a state of collapse, driven by disturbing thoughts and stressful impressions, weary and aching from grappling with all the questions and problems of the day. Everything in me is crying out for rest, rest for the body, rest for the soul. The Jesus Prayer can move me from nervous exhaustion to composure and peace. It is easy to pray. It requires no extra effort for one who is totally worn out or distraught. It sets hallowed, meaningful words on my lips and in my heart, and it puts me at once in touch with my Lord. It is not a demand but a gift.

Or again: someone I meet gives me a touch of joy. There is no need to think up a special prayer to give thanks for it. The gratitude of my heart can be encompassed within the framework of the Jesus Prayer, for it is also a song of praise to the King on high.

Watchfulness and attentiveness in prayer are very much an issue for our times. We find ourselves bombarded with a never-ending torrent of words, impressions, images, people, and thoughts wherever we turn. I open a news-paper, switch on the television, or hop on a bus. I arrive at the schoolroom, the office, the factory, or the kitchen. I am invited perhaps to a friend's house. Perhaps I stand behind the shop counter or at the cash register, meeting the public all day. Perhaps I stand on the corner at rush hour directing the traffic for a couple of hectic hours, half choked by exhaust gases. These are the situations in which, if we are to hold on to our faith, we have to guard against evil and be attentive to Jesus. Guarding the door of our hearts from evil words, idle thoughts, and perverse ideas is vital, and anyone who has not trained himself to do so can easily fall prey to evil spirits.

The whole point of watchfulness at the door of the heart is that we can choose what we think about. We are not mercilessly victimized by the stream of words, thoughts, images, and people that pours in upon us. In the midst of it all we are free, free to choose. Guarding the door of our hearts may look like something negative, but in reality it is wholly positive, it is total freedom. I am not a slave to my own thoughts or to those of other people; I am not a slave to television: I can switch it off. I can also switch off the words in my heart, the things my tongue is saying. I can be silent. I am not a slave to this torrent that comes rushing towards me. I can filter it, I can select. And I am meant to select. We live in a world where we can choose. I can believe in God even if no one else does so. I can pray to Jesus at any time, wherever I am, and no one can prevent my doing so. This is my freedom of religion. Jesus is my master, not all the forces that assail me, trying to make me think as other people think, believe as other people believe, and do what other people do.

By training in the Jesus Prayer I train myself to be out of reach of the attacks of evil on my soul, whether they come from within my own heart or from outside. I have Jesus in my heart, Jesus risen from the dead, and he is more powerful than anything else. To live with him is to have a fortress, a haven of refuge. I may be sacrificing myself for others, pouring myself out for the people I meet and serve. But there is no need that the very heart of my being should be a storm-centre, or a stretch of desert. What is to be there is a temple to the Lord from which praise of the Spirit rings out.

This is why praying the Jesus Prayer also relates us to our fellow men. We are to be Christians for the sake of our neighbours—not in our own power, which is inadequate, but in the power of Christ. We do this not by trying to imitate Christ, but by being transparent for him. When he lives in my heart, then he also shines through; when praise of him is singing in my heart, then it also rings through, often without my knowing. It is not my personality but his that becomes luminous.

Praying the Jesus Prayer also helps me to be watchful and open for Christ's presence in the heart of the other person as well, not just in my own. Attentiveness in this sense is like an aerial, always ready to pick up calls from above, whatever their source. This is why it is so important really to train ourselves both in watchfulness against evil and in receptiveness to Christ.

So it is a good thing that there are people in whose heart Christ dwells. Even one person who has in his heart not a den of thieves but a temple where Christ dwells is an immeasurable blessing for any home, or group, or community. That person carries a lighted candle, the beams of which shine on all whom he meets, on all with whom he has to do. It is not he who shines on the others about him; it is Christ shining in and through him. 'A city set on a hill cannot be hid' (Matt. 5. 14).

Praying the Jesus Prayer docs not lead to unhealthy introversion, to neglect of one's neighbour. It does not lead us to be concerned only with ourselves, looking only at ourselves. There is plenty of criticism today of that kind of Christianity that makes people turn selfishly from the sufferings of the world around us to our own religious concerns. But this criticism does not apply to the Jesus Prayer. On the contrary, this prayer is a prayer of social concern. It makes us light-bearers, Christ-bearers. A lamp is not meant to be put under a bushel, but on a stand, so that it gives light to all, guides them, warms them, encourages them, makes them rejoice, as a light always does. At the same time the Jesus Prayer frees us from thinking about ourselves and makes us Christ-centred. Our thoughts focus not on ourselves but on Christ. When we have nothing else to do, we do not sink into the rut of thinking about either our misfortunes or our successes; instead we turn instinctively to Christ and look to him. Self-pity, bitterness, dislike of others, pride—all are displaced by wonder, love of others, gratitude to Christ, happiness at having him as a friend.

Look at someone carrying a candle. He concentrates on it, on so carrying it that it does not go out. He is not thinking about himself and what he looks like, only about the candle in his hands. Those hands protect the candle against draughts, shield it against attacks. Bearing the light of the world (John 8. 12) in our hearts is like carrying a candle. We forget ourselves in our task, the task of bringing light to a suffering world. At the same time we become *attentive* to the light, watchful against all the attempts by Satan to put it out. Preachers have been known to begin to pray the Jesus Prayer and then to preach more about Jesus than before, often without noticing it themselves, though other people notice it. It is precisely for other people that the light is lit.

But what about this technique of synchronizing our prayer with our breathing? Is that really possible? Is it desirable? Can it not easily lead to our being over-tense, self-centred? Of course this could happen. This is why the *Philokalia* recommends that in all aspects of spiritual life we consult frequently with our spiritual director or counsellor. Probably not everyone can or should practice this co-ordination of breathing with prayer. But it may at least be tried. Perhaps we are walking down a road and breathing steadily and evenly, we can breathe and pray in rhythm. From time to time during the day we can of course consciously pray the Jesus Prayer. But there is a risk involved in praying it disconnected from our breathing—and that is that we may begin thinking about the Prayer rather than praying it. The prayer is so short, and we can think it through so quickly. Co-ordinating it with the breath does one good thing for the person praying: it gives the prayer a more natural rhythm and pulse. The whole question of the time and pulse of the prayer may well be considered by persons beginning to pray the Jesus Prayer. Breathing at the same time as we pray gives this very short prayer a surer length and duration. Then the prayer is neither forced nor prayed carelessly. It carries us when we pray it as gently as does our own breathing when we inhale and exhale. The prayer is the breath of the Christian life.

The Bible closes with another form of the Jesus Prayer. The last chapter of the Book of Revelation, in the last verse but one, has a prayer that is really worth using: 'Come, Lord Jesus!'

For the early church the titles Lord and Christ were one and the same: he who is Lord or King is he who is the Anointed, the Christ. To pray that the Lord Jesus will come is to pray that Jesus Christ, my Lord, may come. This form of the Jesus Prayer is easy to remember. We do not have to get ourselves into a certain mood before we can pray it. We do not need to have a prayer book at hand. This prayer of the primitive church looks forward to the return of Christ at the last day; it is at the centre of our faith, a prayer of devotion. It speaks of our deepest longing for Christ and our love for him. It can be prayed by the whole congregation and by individuals. It is good to use when we are tired and cannot manage many words. It has within it a note of both praise and worship. In this simple prayer our earliest fellow-believers were showing us the way, a path away from artificial and unnatural striving for effect in the spiritual life, a path towards what is understandable in daily life and truly close to reality. There is no way of saying it more simply: 'Come, Lord Jesus'.

There have always been, and still are, Christians who 'talk with Jesus' quite naturally, as with a present friend. A country pastor once went to visit an old lady who lived on a farm. He got no answer to his knock at the kitchen door, so he walked out into the garden where he found her standing still under a tree. When she saw him, she said quietly: 'Would you mind waiting just a moment? I'm talking with Jesus.' Many of the hymns which sing on in our heads after worship are a kind of Jesus Prayer.

> Jesus, of thee shall be my song,
> To thee my heart and soul belong;
> All that I have or am in thine,
> And thou, blest Saviour, thou art mine.
> Jesus, my Lord, I thee adore,
> O make me love thee more and more.[1]

[1] H. Collins, *Hymns Ancient and Modern Revised*, no. 202.

So too some of the sprightlier revivalist hymns convey just what the Jesus Prayer is meant to be:

A little talk with Jesus make it right, all right:
   In trials of every kind,
   Praise God, I always find
A little talk with Jesus makes it right, all right.[1]

Indeed, in the literature of prayer we find instances that almost exactly match the content of the classic Jesus Prayer. One that comes immediately to mind for me is this prayer:[2]

O Holy Spirit
Make my heart a shrine for the words of eternal life.
Keep from me the tumult of the busy world,
And bid desires be still.
Create a holy silence in my heart,
That I may hear the voice of the Eternal.

O Holy Spirit
Make my heart a dwelling place for the Lord of my life.
I need him, not just as one who visits me,
But as one who abides in my heart and never leaves it.

O Holy Spirit
Make my heart a chamber for prayer.
Help me to worship God
With words and wordlessly, day and night,
So that his praise is ever on my lips
Till I am wholly sanctified.

Amen.

[1] H. Wright, *C.S.S.M. Choruses*. no. 1.
[2] W. Ruding, *Den Svenska Bönboken*, no. 664.

Bible Passages

94